MW01063021

Little Office

of the

Blessed Virgin Mary

GS

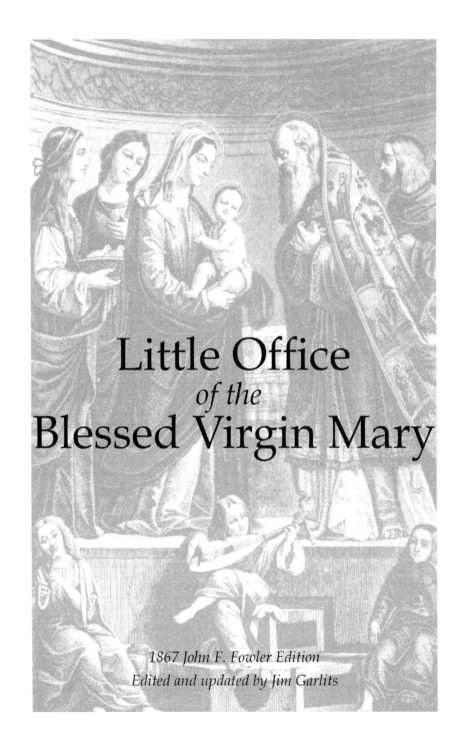

Little Office
of the
Blessed Virgin Mary

1867 John F. Fowler Edition
Edited and updated by Jim Garlits

Table of Contents

NOTE

This "Little Office" of the Blessed Virgin Mary is from the 1867 edition originally published by John F. Fowler, 3 Crow Street, Dublin, Ireland. Slight modifications aided clarity.

Those of us who are beholden to Our Lady will appreciate that this short prayer allows them not only to bless the day but also to do it using a text that is at once reverent and readable; its elevated language exemplifies noble simplicity and unembellished piety, in the most beautiful tradition of good liturgical prayer. It is accessible to those attached to the Extraordinary and Ordinary Forms.

My hope is that Our Lady will be pleased to hear again this particular form of the little office on the lips of her children. My prayer is that it might bring you closer to her divine Son, fortify you for daily battle with the Enemy, and sustain you as you tend the fields of your apostolate.

Jim Garlits

BACKGROUND

The Little Office of the Blessed Virgin Mary is of ancient usage in the Church, and was recited by the clergy and devout laity, and practiced by rule in religious monasteries, even from the sixth and seventh centuries, and probably at a more early period, as Meratus observes in his annotations on Gavantus.

This Office was instituted by the Church, guided by the Spirit of God, and is divided into seven canonical hours, according to the following order, set down in the Roman Breviary:

Vespers
Compline
Matins with Lauds
Prime
Terce
Sext
None

These canonical terms should be adopted in naming the hours. The Little Office of the Blessed Virgin Mary is always of a simple rite, and as such, it should be recited every day, and invariably observed the whole year round. The simple rite signifies first, that the office commences at Vespers, and terminates at None. Second, that *there be said only one nocturn at Matins*, the psalms are changed according to the order of the days, third, that there be recited the common suffrage, or commemoration for the saints, after the prayer in Vespers and Lauds; and fourth, that the anthems of the psalms be simple, or that the first words only of the anthems be said before the psalms, but after the psalms the anthems recited entire.

It is therefore a material fault in Church rites to subject the Little Office of the Blessed Virgin Mary to the various changes of rites and ceremonies of what is called the Divine Office and to recite the anthems entire before the psalms on feasts of a double rite; for the Office of the Blessed Virgin Mary has no relation to the occurring festivals and transferred feasts of the Divine Office. The contrary practice is erroneous, and should be corrected, because it is repugnant to the sacred rite and order prescribed by the Church. Besides, there are many rubrical difficulties and absurdities that would arise by changing 'thus the simple rite of the Little Office of the Blessed Virgin Mary.

The anthems, prayers, and lessons of this Office are changed at different times in the year, as in Advent, at Christmas time, in Paschal time, and the rest of the year. These changes are marked in the Office by the time of the year printed in Italic type, included between a parenthesis, as may be observed by the devout reader. The office in Advent begins at Vespers on Saturday before the first Sunday of Advent, until None on Christmas Eve. The Office at Christmas time begins at Vespers on the vigil of Christmas, until Vespers on the second of February, feast of the Purification of the Blessed Virgin Mary. The common Office begins at Matins on the second of February, till None on Saturday before the first Sunday in Advent. Paschal time is from Vespers on Easter Saturday, till None on Saturday in Whitsun week before Trinity Sunday.

The hymn "Te Deum" is not prescribed to be said in the Little Office of the Blessed Virgin Mary, but as this is a devotional practice introduced in the Office, it may be said after the third lesson of the Nocturn all times of the year, except during Advent, and from Septuagesima Sunday until Easter. It may be likewise said on the feasts of the Blessed Virgin Mary in Advent and Lent, that is, on the 8th and 18th of December, on the 25th of March, and on the second of February, when it comes after Septuagesima Sunday.

Note: First, when these days fall on Sunday, the Te Deum is said in the Sunday office and not on the following Mondays, although the feast of the Blessed Virgin Mary may be transferred to Monday in the Divine Office on account of the privileged Sundays. Second, as the Matins for the day are usually said in the preceding evening, this hymn is then added to the office.

Vespers and Complin are usually said in the late afternoon, Matins with Lauds late in the evening, or both Vespers, and Matins can be recited together late in the evening for the convenience of those who cannot attend them in choir more early on account of business and the lesser hours of Prime, etc. are said in the morning.

In order to promote true piety towards the Blessed Virgin Mary and to encourage the devout recital of her Office, Pope Pius V granted to those who are bound to say her Little Office the indulgence[1] of a hundred days every time they perform this duty

1   Changed to a partial indulgence, as opposed to a plenary indulgence, in the new *Enchiridion.*

at the prescribed times, according to Church rites. His Holiness has also granted fifty days of indulgence to those who are not bound to this office, each time they devoutly recite the Little Office of the Blessed Virgin Mary.

Rubrics

1. When Lauds are said immediately after Matins, the Ave Maria before the V. *Deus in adjutorium*, is omitted.

2. If the Office be said in private, the anthem of the Blessed Virgin is said after Lauds and Complin only; when the office is interrupted at the end of Prime, Terce, Sext, None, or Vespers, an Our Father is said; Complin is always concluded with an Our Father, Hail Mary, and the Creed.

3. When the office is said without interruption, the anthem of the Blessed Virgin is not said after Lands, Prime, Terce, Sext, and None, but only at the last hour.

4. The hymn *Te Deum* may be said, or not, at will from Christmas to Septuagesima Sunday, and from Easter to Advent. During Advent, and from Septuagesima Sunday to Easter, the *Te Deum* is only said on feasts of the Blessed Virgin.

5. On the feast of the Annunciation, the Office is said as in Advent.

6. The *Te Deum* is said on the feast of the Purification, even though it fall after Septuagesima Sunday: if this feast be transferred, the change of office is transferred too.

7. From Septuagesima Sunday to Vespers on Holy Saturday the Alleluia is never said. During Passion and Holy Weeks the Gloria Patri is never omitted.

8. During Paschal time Alleluia is not added to the Invitatory, Versicles or Responses.

9. In this office, when a commemoration is made of a patron saint, it should be at Vespers and Lauds, between the prayer which follows the anthems of the *Magnificat* and *Benedictus*, and the Commemoration of Saints, *Sancti Dei Omnes*, or *Ecce Dominus Veniet*.

10. The office for the year begins at the Matins of the day after the Purification.

11. The Office for Advent' begins with the Vespers of the Saturday before the first Sunday in Advent.

12. The office for Christmas begins with the Vespers of Christmas Eve, and continues until the Vespers of the Purification inclusively.

13. The anthem *Regina Cæli*, after the three canticles is said for the first time at the *Nunc Dimmitis* on Holy Saturday, and for the last, at Lauds on the Saturday before Trinity Sunday.

BEFORE & AFTER PRAYERS

Before the Office

Open thou, O Lord, my mouth to bless thy holy name. Cleanse my heart from all vain, perverse, and distracting thoughts, enlighten my understanding, inflame my will, that I may worthily perform this Little Office and may deserve to be heard in the presence of thy divine Majesty: Through Christ our Lord, Amen.

I offer up to thee these hours, and unite my intention with that of Jesus Christ, thy Son, who, while on earth, rendered you the most acceptable homage of divine praises.

Hail, Mary, full of grace, the Lord is with thee: Blessed art thou among women and blessed is the fruit of thy womb, Jesus. Holy Mary, Mother of God, pray for us sinners, now, and in the hour of our death. Amen.

After the Office

Everlasting praise, honor, power, and glory be given by all creatures to the most holy and undivided Trinity, to the Humanity of our crucified Lord Jesus Christ, to the fruitful purity of the most blessed and most glorious Mary ever Virgin, and to the company of all the Saints; and may we obtain the remission of all our sins through all eternity. Amen.

V. Blessed is the womb of the Virgin Mary that bore the Son of the eternal Father.

R. And blessed be the paps that gave suck to Christ our Lord.

Our Father…
Hail Mary…
I believe in God…

INVITATORY

Twice repeated antiphon

Antiphon: Hail Mary full of grace, the Lord is with thee.

Psalm 95: Venite Exultamus

Come, let us rejoice in the Lord, let us joyfully cry out to God our Savior: let us present ourselves before him, to celebrate his praises, and to sing with joy canticles unto him.

> *Hail, Mary, full of grace, the Lord is with thee.*

Because God is a mighty Lord and a great King above all gods; for the Lord will not reject his people; in his hand are all the bounds of the earth, and he looks down on the heights of the mountains.

> *The Lord is with thee.*

The sea is his; for he made it, and his hands framed the earth; come then, let us adore, and fall prostrate before God, let us weep in the presence of the Lord who made us, because he is the Lord our God; we are his people, and the sheep of his pasture.

> *Hail, Mary, full of grace, the Lord is with thee.*

If this day you should hear his voice, harden not your hearts, as you did when you provoked him, on the day you offended him in the desert; where your fathers tempted me, they tried and saw my works.

> *The Lord is with thee.*

I was forty years with this race of men, and said: The hearts of this people are always wandering, but they have not known my ways; and I swore to them in my wrath, that they should not enter my abode of rest.

Hail, Mary, full of grace, the Lord is with thee.

Glory be to the Father, and to the Son, and to the Holy Ghost. As it was in the beginning, is now, and ever shall be, world without end. Amen.

The Lord is with thee.

Antiphon: Hail, Mary, full of grace, the Lord is with thee.

MATINS & LAUDS

Being "nocturns" these two hours are recited before sunrise.

Matins

O Divine and adorable Lord Jesus Christ, who have graciously redeemed us by your bitter passion and death, we offer up these Matins and Lauds to your honor and glory, and most humbly beseech you, through the vile treatment you received from the Jews, who dragged you to the courts of impious High priests, where you were falsely accused, struck in the face, called a blasphemer, and declared guilty of death, and suffered most cruel torments with blows, bruises, and unheard-of injuries, during the whole night, to grant us resignation and silence during all calumnies, detractions, and sufferings for the love of you, and to give us grace never to return injury for injury, but to practice that truly Christian revenge of overcoming evil with good, to do good to those who hate us, to bless those who curse us, and to pray for those who persecute and calumniate us. Amen.

Hail Mary, full of grace, the Lord is with thee. Blessed art thou amongst women and blessed is the fruit of thy womb, Jesus. Holy Mary, Mother of God, pray for us sinners, now and at the hour of our death. Amen.

V. O Lord, open thou my lips.
R. And my mouth shall declare thy praise
V. Incline unto my aid, O God.
R. O Lord, make haste to help me.

Glory be to the Father, and to the Son, and to the Holy Ghost. As it was in the beginning, is now, and ever shall be, world

13

without end. Amen, Alleluia.

During Lent: *Praise be to thee, O Lord, king of eternal glory.*

Hymn

The sovereign God, whose hands sustain
the globe of heaven, the earth and main,
Adored and praised by each degree,
Lies hid, O Sacred Maid, in thee.

He, whom the sun and moon obey,
To whom all creatures' homage pay;
The Judge of men and angels' doom,
Resides within thy virgin womb.

O Happy Mary, chose to bear
Thy Maker's co-eternal Heir;
Whose fingers span this earth around,
Whose arms the whole creation bound.

The angel's voice pronounced thee blest,
the Holy Ghost on thee did rest;
To us thou didst bestow by birth
The most desired of heaven and earth.

To thee, O Jesus, Mary's son,
Be everlasting homage done;
To God the Father we repeat
The same, and to the Paraclete. Amen.

ON SUNDAY, MONDAY, AND THURSDAY

Antiphon: Blessed art thou among women; and blessed is the fruit of thy womb.

Psalm 8. Domine Dominus Noster.

O Lord, our sovereign Lord, how wonderful is thy name over the whole earth! For thy grandeur is exalted above the heavens. Thou hast received due praise from the mouths of infants and sucklings, to confound thy enemies, and to destroy the spirit of hatred and vengeance.

For I shall consider the heavens, which are the work of thy hands; the moon and stars, which thou has formed; what is man, that thou art mindful of him, or the son of man, that thou dost visit him?

Thou hast created him a little inferior to the angels, thou hast crowned him with honor and glory and gave him dominion over all the works of thy hands.

Thou hast rendered all things subject to him, the sheep, and the oxen, and also the cattle of the field;
The birds of the air and the fishes of the sea, and all that glide through the course of the waters. O Lord, our sovereign Lord, how wonderful is thy name over the whole earth!

Glory be to the Father, and to the Son, and to the Holy Ghost. As it was in the beginning, is now, and ever shall be, world without end. Amen.

Antiphon: Blessed art thou among women; and blessed is the fruit of thy womb.

Antiphon: Like choice myrrh, thou hast rendered a most fragrant odor, O holy Mother of God.

Psalm 19: Caeli Enarrant.

The heavens display the glory of God, and the firmament publishes the works of his hands. Each day announces his word to the following day, and each night declares his knowledge to the succeeding night. There are no tongues or languages, where their voices are not heard. Their eloquence went forth through the whole world, and their words have reached the bounds of the earth.

The glory of his abode is fulgent like the Sun, and he is adorned like the bridegroom going out of his chamber.
He proceedeth with joy like a giant on his way; his coming forth begins from the summit of heaven, and he continues his course to the end thereof: there is not one who can abscond from his rays.

The law of the Lord is perfect, it converts souls: the words of the Lord are faithful, and give wisdom to the humble. The ordinances of the Lord are righteous, rejoicing the hearts: the precept of the Lord is luminous, and enlightens our understanding. The fear of the Lord is holy, and continues forevermore: the judgments of the Lord are founded on truth and justice.

They are more desirable than gold or precious stones, and sweeter than the honey and honeycomb. For thy servant observeth them; and they who keep them, find an ample recompense.

Who can comprehend what sin is? Cleanse me from my hidden sins, and from those of others save thy servant. If they shall not be imputed to me, I will be then pure and will be free from the very great guilt of sin. Then shall my prayer be directed to please thee: and my interior meditation be always made in thy presence. O Lord, thou art my help and my Redeemer.

Glory be to the Father, and to the Son, and to the Holy Ghost. As it was in the beginning, is now, and ever shall be, world without end. Amen.

Antiphon: Like choice myrrh, thou has rendered a most fragrant odor, O holy Mother of God.

* * * * * * * * * *

Antiphon: In honor of this most chase Virgin let us sing canticles with sweet harmony.

Psalm 24: Domini Est Terra.

The Lord possesses the earth, and all that it contains: he owns the whole world and all its inhabitants, for he hath founded it on the seas, and hath raised it over the surface of the rivers.

Who shall ascend on the mount of the Lord, and who shall dwell in his holy sanctuary? Those who do no harm, and are pure of heart; who give not their hearts to vain desires, nor deceives his neighbor by false oaths. He shall receive the blessing of the Lord, and mercy from God his Savior.

Such is the inheritance of those who truly seek him, who desire the presence of the God of Jacob.
Open wide your gates, O ye princes, and let the eternal doors be thrown open, and the King of Glory shall make his entrance. Who is this King of glory? He is the valiant and mighty Lord, the Lord who has triumphed in battle.
Open wide your gates, O ye princes, let the eternal gates be thrown open, and the King of glory shall make his entrance.

Who is this King of glory? The Lord of hosts is this king of glory.

Glory be to the Father, and to the Son, and to the Holy Ghost. As it was in the beginning, is now, and ever shall be, world without end. Amen.

Antiphon: In honor of this most chase Virgin let us sing canticles with sweet harmony.

V. Grace is spread on thy lips.
R. Therefore God has blessed thee forever.

Our Father, &c.

Proceed to page 27

ON TUESDAY AND FRIDAY

Antiphon: In thy comeliness and thy beauty go on, proceed prosperously, and reign.

Psalm 45: Eructavit Cor Meum.

My heart is ready to declare grand things: I will devote my works to the King of kings. My tongue shall follow his inspiration, like a quick pen of an able scrivener.

O thou most beautiful among the sons of men, grace is spread on thy lips. Therefore God hath blessed thee forever. Gird thyself with thy sword, O thou most Mighty. In thy comeliness and thy beauty, go on, proceed prosperously, and reign.

For the sake of truth, of meekness, and of justice; and thy right hand shall conduct thee wonderfully.
Thy arrows are sharp, under thee shall people fall: they shall pierce the hearts of the king's enemies.
Thy throne, O God, is an eternal reign: the scepter of thy empire is a scepter of equity.

Thou hast loved justice, and hated iniquity; therefore the Lord thy God anointed thee with the oil of joy above all thy partners. Myrrh, and aloes, and cassia perfume thy robes, and thy ivory palaces: where the daughters of the king have the honor to entertain thee.

The queen on thy right hand in vesture trimmed with gold, and variegated with ornaments. Hearken, my daughter, and see and incline thy ear, forget thy people, and thy father's house. And the king will be enamored with thy beauty, for he is the Lord thy God, and the people will adore him. And the daughters of Tyre shall offer gifts; yea the rich nobility too will come to render thee their vows. All the glory of the king's daughter is in her interior; although she be decorated with fringes of gold and embroideries.

Virgins shall be conducted in her retinue to the king: her neighbors shall be brought to thee. They shall be accompanied with joy and delights: and shall be introduced into the temple of the king.

Thou art blessed with children to hold the place of thy fathers: thou wilt appoint them princes over the whole earth. They shall be mindful of thy name, through succession of ages. Therefore shall the people praise thee forever, yea for evermore.

Glory be to the Father, and to the Son, and to the Holy Ghost. As it was in the beginning, is now, and ever shall be, world without end. Amen.

Antiphon: In thy comeliness and thy beauty go on, proceed prosperously, and reign.

* * * * * * * * * *

Antiphon: God will assist her with his presence. God is in the midst of her; she shall not be disturbed.

Psalm 46: *Deus Noster Refugium*

God is our refuge and strength; he is our helper in afflictions, which have heavily fallen on us. So we shall have nothing to fear when the earth will be troubled, and the mountains transported into the depth of the sea. The waters roared, and were disturbed: and their impetuous torrent made the mountains tremble.

A current of heavenly joy overflows the city of God: the

Most High hath sanctified his own tabernacle. God is in the midst thereof, it shall not be disturbed: the Lord will protect it from the dawn of the morning. Nations are disturbed, and kingdoms have tottered: the earth trembled at his voice. The Lord of hosts is with us: the God of Jacob is our protector.

Come and behold the works of the Lord, and the prodigies he wrought on earth: he makes the wars cease, even to the bounds of the earth. He shall destroy the bow, and break the weapons, and cast the shields into the fire. Consider, and know that I am the Lord: I shall rule over nations, and shall be great on earth. The Lord of hosts is with us: the God of Jacob is our protector.

Glory be to the Father, and to the Son, and to the Holy Ghost. As it was in the beginning, is now, and ever shall be, world without end. Amen.

Antiphon: God will assist her with his presence. God is in the midst of her, she shall not be disturbed.

* * * * * * * * * *

Antiphon: We all shall truly rejoice, if we are constantly devoted to thee, O holy Mother of God.

Psalm 87: Fundamenta Ejus

Sion is founded on holy mountains; the Lord is pleased with its gates above all the tabernacles of Jacob. Glorious things are spoken of thee, O city of God. I shall be mindful of Rahab and Babylon, to whom I will make myself known. Behold the Philistines and Tyre, and the inhabitants of Ethiopia: these shall be there.

Shall not Sion say: A man is born in her, and this man is the

Most High, who founded her? The Lord shall relate in the records of the people and of princes, the names of those who have dwelt therein.

All shall truly rejoice, who abide in thee.

Glory be to the Father, and to the Son, and to the Holy Ghost. As it was in the beginning, is now, and ever shall be, world without end. Amen.

Antiphon: We all shall truly rejoice, if we are constantly devoted to thee, O holy Mother of God.

V. Grace is spread on thy lips.
R. Therefore God has blessed thee forever.

Our Father, &c.

Proceed to page 27

ON WEDNESDAY AND SATURDAY

Antiphon: Rejoice, O Virgin Mary, thou alone has rendered the Church triumphant over all the heresies spread through the earth.

Psalm 96: Cantate Domino.

Sing to the Lord a new canticle: let the whole earth chant the praises of the Lord. Sing to the Lord, and bless his holy name: proclaim each day the good tidings of salvation. Publish his glory among the Gentiles, and his wonderful works among the people. For the Lord is great, and most worthy of all praise: he is to be feared above all the gods of the earth. Because all the gods of the Gentiles are devils: but our Lord has formed the heavens above.

Glory and beauty belong to him; holiness and grandeur decorate his sanctuary. Bring to the Lord, ye kindred of the Gentiles, render to the Lord glory and honor: give that glory due to the name of the Lord. Prepare sacrifices, and enter into his courts: adore the Lord in his holy sanctuary. Let the earth be moved at his presence: announce it to the nations: Behold the Lord reigneth.

For he hath established order on the earth, which shall not be disturbed: the Lord will judge all people according to the truth of his holy law. May the heavens rejoice, and may the earth, the sea, and all its fullness exult in transports of joy: may the country around, and what it contains, be animated with gladness.

Then shall all the trees of the forests be revested with delight before the presence of the Lord, because he cometh: for he is come to judge the earth. He will judge the world with justice, and all the people according to the truth of his holy law.

Glory be to the Father, and to the Son, and to the Holy Ghost. As it was in the beginning, is now, and ever shall be, world without end. Amen.

Antiphon: Rejoice, O Virgin Mary, thou alone has rendered the Church triumphant over all the heresies spread through the earth.

* * * * * * * * * *

Antiphon: Vouchsafe that I may praise thee, O sacred Virgin, obtain for me strength against my enemies.

Psalm 97: *Dominus Regnavit.*

The Lord hath reigned, let the earth rejoice: and may gladness be spread through many islands.
Clouds and darkness are around him: justice and equity are the basis of his throne. A flame of fire shall precede him, and shall consume around all his enemies. His lightnings flash throughout the world: the earth saw the light and was moved to fear.

The mountains have melted away at the presence of the Lord, like wax before the fire; the whole earth too has trembled at his presence. The heavens have declared his righteousness, and all the people have beheld his glory. May they all be confounded who adore graven things: and who glory in their idols.

Adore him, all ye his angels: Sion hath heard his voice and was filled with gladness. And the daughters of Judah have rejoiced, on account of thy judgments, O Lord. Because thou,

O Lord, art most high above all the earth: thou art exceedingly exalted above all gods.

All you who love the Lord, detest evil; the Lord watcheth over the souls of his Saints and will deliver them from the power of sinners. Light is risen for the just, and joy for the upright of heart.
Ye just, rejoice in the Lord and render glory to the author of all sanctity.

Glory be to the Father, and to the Son, and to the Holy Ghost. As it was in the beginning, is now, and ever shall be, world without end. Amen.

Antiphon: Vouchsafe that I may praise thee, O sacred Virgin, obtain for me strength against thy enemies.

* * * * * * * * * *

(Through the year) Antiphon: After thy child-birth thou didst remain an inviolate virgin, O Mother of God: make intercession for us.

(In Advent) Antiphon: The Angel of the Lord declared unto Mary, and she conceived by the Holy Ghost, Alleluia.

Psalm 98: Cantate Domino.

Sing to the Lord a new canticle; because he has wrought many wonderful things. His strong hand has effected salvation, and also his divine power. The Lord hath made known the promised Savior: he hath revealed his righteousness before the nations. He hath been mindful of his mercy, and of the inviolable promises he made Israel.

All the boundaries of the earth have beheld the salvation

which our God has wrought. Let the whole earth praise God with joy, may it chant forth, and rejoice, and sing canticles to him. Sing praises to the Lord on the harp, with the melody of the psalter; on the metal trumpet, accompanied with the music of the cornet.

Make joyful harmony before the Lord our king: may the sea, and all its fullness, may the earth, and its inhabitants, be moved to exultation. The rivers shall applaud, the mountains too shall rejoice before the Lord: for he cometh to judge the earth. He will judge the world with justice, and all the people according to the truth of his holy law.

Glory be to the Father, and to the Son, and to the Holy Ghost. As it was in the beginning, is now, and ever shall be, world without end. Amen.

(Through the year) Antiphon: After thy child-birth thou didst remain an inviolate virgin, O Mother of God, make intercession for us.

(In Advent) Antiphon: The Angel of the Lord declared unto Mary, and she conceived by the Holy Ghost, Alleluia.

V. Grace is spread on thy lips.
R. Therefore God hath blessed thee forever.

(In silence) Our Father, &c.

V. And lead us not into temptation.
R. But deliver us from evil. Amen.

Absolution.

By the prayers and merits of the ever blessed Virgin Mary, and of all the saints, may the Lord bring us to the kingdom of heaven.

R. Amen.

V. (If led by a priest) Pray, father, give me your blessing.

The Blessing: May the Virgin Mary obtain for us the blessing of her divine Son. Amen.

THE LESSONS

These following Lessons are recited throughout the year, except during Advent.

The first Lesson. Ecclesiasticus 24: 11-14

I sought everywhere for a place of rest, and I shall dwell in the inheritance of the Lord. Then the Creator of the universe hath given me orders, and spoke unto me: He, who has created me, reposed in my tabernacle and said to me: Let thy dwelling be in Jacob, and thy inheritance in Israel, and take root among my elect. But thou, O Lord, have mercy on us.

R. Thanks be to God.

R. O holy and immaculate Virginity, I know not with what praises to extol thy dignity: because whom the heavens could not contain, thou hast borne in thy womb.

V. Blessed are thou among women, and blessed is the fruit of thy womb.
R. Because whom the heavens could not contain, thou hast borne in thy womb.

V. (If led by a priest) Pray, father, give me your blessing.

R. The Blessing: May the Virgin of virgins make intercession for us to the Lord.

The Second Lesson. Ecclesiasticus 24:15-16

I have likewise dwelt in Sion, and have rested in the holy city, and my power was strengthened in Jerusalem. I settled myself among a people whom the Lord hath honored, and hath chosen for his portion and inheritance, and have fixed my abode in the company of all the saints. But thou, O Lord, have mercy on us.

R. Thanks be to God.

R. Blessed art thou, O Virgin Mary, who has borne the Lord and Creator of the world: Thou hast brought forth him who made thee, and remainest ever a virgin.

V. Hail, Mary, full of grace, the Lord is with thee.
R. Thou hast brought forth him who made thee, and remainest ever a virgin.

When the Te Deum is said after the third Lesson, the last verse of this Responsory is again repeated, thus:

Glory be to the Father, and to the Son, and to the Holy Ghost.

R. Thou hast brought forth him who made thee, and remainest ever a virgin.

V. (If led by a priest) Pray, father, give me your blessing.

R. The Blessing: May the Lord, through the intercession of the Virgin Mother, grant us salvation and peace.
R. Amen.

Matins

The Third Lesson: Ecclesiasticus 24:17-20

I am exalted like the cedar on Lebanon, and as the cypress tree on Mount Sion: I have grown like the palm tree in Cades, and as the rose plant in Jericho: I have flourished like a fair olive tree in the fields, and as a plane tree watered by the stream. I yielded forth a fragrant smell like cinnamon and aromatic balm: and, like the best myrrh, I spread around the sweetest odor. But thou, O Lord, have mercy upon us.

R. Thanks be to God.

The following Responsory is omitted when the Te Deum is said.

R. Thou art truly happy, O sacred Virgin Mary, and most worthy of all praise: Because out of thee is risen the Sun of righteousness, Jesus Christ, our God.

V. Pray for the people, intercede for the clergy, and plead for the devout: let all be sensible of thine aid, who celebrate thy holy memory.

R. Because of thee is risen the Sun of righteousness, Jesus Christ, our God.

Glory be to the Father, and to the Son, and to the Holy Ghost.
R. Jesus Christ, our God.

TE DEUM

Thee, sovereign God, our grateful accents praise;
We own thee Lord, and bless thy wondrous ways.
To thee, eternal Father, earth's whole frame
With loudest trumpets sounds immortal fame;

Lord, God of Hosts! For thee the heavenly powers
With sounding antiphons fill the vaulted towers;
Thy Cherubim, thy Seraphim, thrice holy, cry:
To thee, O God, who dwells and reigns on high.

Both heaven and earth thy majesty display.
They owe their beauty to thy glorious ray.
Thy praises fill the loud apostles' choir.
The train of prophets in the song conspire.

Red hosts of martyrs in the chorus shine,
And vocal blood with vocal music join.
By these thy Church, inspired with heavenly art,
Around the world maintains a second part;

And tunes her sweetest notes, O God, for thee,
The Father of unbounded majesty,
The Son, adored co-partner of thy seat,
And equal everlasting Paraclete.

Thou King of Glory, Christ of the Most High,

Thou co-eternal filial Deity;
Thou, who to save the world's impending doom,
Vouchsafest to dwell within a virgin's womb.

Old tyrant Death disarmed, before thee flew,
The bolts of heaven and back the foldings drew,
To give access, and make the faithful way,
From God's right hand thy filial beams display.

Thou art to judge the living and the dead;
Then spare those souls for whom thy veins have bled.

(Genuflect)

O take us up amongst the blessed above,
To share with them in thy eternal love.

Preserve, O Lord, thy people, and enhance,
Thy blessing on thy own inheritance.
Forever raise their hearts, and rule their ways;
Each day we bless thee, and proclaim thy praise.

No age shall fail to celebrate thy name,
Nor hour neglect thy everlasting fame.
Preserve our souls, O Lord, this day from ill:
Have mercy on us, Lord, have mercy still.

As we have hoped, do thou reward our pain:
We've hoped in thee, let not us hope in vain.

Lessons In Advent

After the Psalms of the Nocturn, according to the order of the day, the following prayers and lessons are said:

(In silence) Our Father, &c.
V. And lead us not into temptation.
R. But deliver us from evil.

Absolution.

By the prayers and merits of the ever blessed Virgin Mary, and of all the Saints, may the Lord bring us to the kingdom of heaven.

R. Amen.

V. (If led by a priest) Pray, father, give me your blessing.

The blessing: May the Virgin Mary obtain for us the blessing of her divine Son.

R. Amen.

The first Lesson: Luke 1:26-28

The angel Gabriel was sent by God to a city of Galilee, called Nazareth, to a virgin espoused to a man, whose name was Joseph, of the house of David: and the virgin's name was Mary. And the angel having entered, said unto her: Hail, full of grace, the Lord is with thee: blessed art thou among women. But thou, O Lord, have mercy on us.

R. Thanks be to God.

R. The angel Gabriel was sent to the Virgin Mary, espoused to Joseph, to announce to her the divine message; but the light of his countenance affrighted the sacred Virgin. Do not fear, Mary, thou hast found grace with the Lord: Behold, thou shalt conceive, and bring forth a Son, who shall be called the Son of the Most High.

V. The Lord God shall give him the throne of his father David, and he shall eternally reign over the house of Jacob.

R. Behold, thou shalt conceive, and bring forth a Son, who shall be called the Son of the Most High.

V. (If led by a priest): Pray, father, give me your blessing.

R. The Blessing: May the Virgin of virgins make intercession for us to the Lord.

R. Amen.

The second Lesson: Luke 1:29-33

Mary having heard these words, was much troubled, and reflected on what kind of salutation this could be. And the angel said to her: Do not fear, Mary, for thou hast found grace with God: behold, thou shalt conceive in thy womb, and shalt bring forth a Son, and shalt call his name Jesus. He shall be great and shall be called the Son of the Most High: the Lord God will give him the throne of his father David, and he shall eternally reign over the house of Jacob, and of his kingdom, there shall be no end. But thou, O Lord, have mercy on us.

R. Thanks be to God.

R. Hail, Mary, full of grace: the Lord is with thee. The Holy Ghost shall descend on thee, and the virtue of the Most High shall overshadow thee: for the Holy One, who will be born of thee, shall be called the Son of God.

V. How shall this be done, because I know not man? The angel answering, said to her:
R. The Holy Ghost shall descend on thee, and the virtue of the Most High shall overshadow thee: For the Holy One, who will be born of thee, shall be called the Son of God.

V. (If led by a priest) Pray, father, give me your blessing.

R. The Blessing: May the Lord, through the intercession of the Virgin Mother, grant us salvation and peace.

R. Amen.

The third Lesson: Luke 1:34-38

Then Mary said to the angel: How shall this be done, for I know not man? The angel answered her: The Holy Ghost shall descend on thee, and the virtue of the Most High shall overshadow thee: therefore the Holy One, who will be born of thee, shall be called the Son of God, and behold, thy cousin Elizabeth hath conceived a son in her old age; and this month is the sixth to her, who is called barren; for with God nothing shall be impossible. Mary then replied: Behold the handmaid of the Lord, be it done to me according to thy word. But thou, O Lord, have mercy on us.

R. Thanks be to God.

R. Receive, O Virgin Mary, the word which the Lord declared to thee by the ministry of the angel: thou shalt conceive, and bring forth a Son, who will be both God and man: That thou mayest be called blessed among women.

V. Thou shalt bring forth a son, and shalt suffer no detriment in thy virginity: thou shalt become a mother without ceasing to be a chaste virgin.

R. That thou mayest be called blessed among all women.

V. Glory be to the Father, and to the Son, and to the Holy Ghost.

R. That thou mayest be called blessed among all women.

On feasts of the Blessed Virgin Mary, the Te Deum may be said: then the last Responsory is omitted, the Glory Be is added to the second Responsory, and the last Versicle is again repeated.

LAUDS

Hail Mary, full of grace: the Lord is with thee. Blessed art thou amongst women, and blessed is the fruit of thy womb, Jesus. Holy Mary, Mother of God, pray for us sinners, now and at the hour of our death. Amen.

V. Incline unto my aid, O God.
R. O Lord, make haste to help me.

Glory be to the Father, and to the Son, and to the Holy Ghost. As it was in the beginning, is now, and ever shall be, world without end. Amen.

During Lent: Praise be to thee, O Lord, king of eternal glory.

(Throughout the year) Antiphon: Mary is taken up into heaven; the angels rejoice in her glory, and with praises bless the Lord.

(In Advent) Antiphon: The angel Gabriel was sent to the Virgin Mary, espoused to Joseph.

(Christmas time) Antiphon: O admirable intercourse! The creator of mankind, assuming a body animated with a soul, was pleased to be born of a virgin; and becoming man, without human concurrence, he made us partakers of his divine nature.

Psalm 93: Dominus Regnavit.

The Lord hath reigned, and is clothed with beauty: he is

covered with strength, and well girded, for he hath founded the earth on its basis, which shall not be disturbed. Thy throne was prepared before the world: thou art from eternity.

The floods have risen, O Lord: the floods have roared aloud. The rivers have swelled their waves: their roaring is the noise of many waters.
Wonderful are the surges of the sea: but more wonderful is the Lord who rules over all things.
Thy testimonies are become exceedingly credible: holiness becometh thy house, O Lord, unto length of days.

Glory be to the Father, and to the Son, and to the Holy Ghost. As it was in the beginning, is now, and ever shall be, world without end. Amen.

(Throughout the year) Antiphon: Mary is taken up into heaven; the angels rejoice in her glory, and with praises bless the Lord.

(In Advent) Antiphon: The angel Gabriel was sent to the Virgin Mary, espoused to Joseph.

(Christmas time) Antiphon: O admirable intercourse! the creator of mankind, assuming a body animated with a soul, was pleased to be born of a virgin; and becoming man, without human concurrence, he made us partakers of his divine nature.

* * * * * * * * * *

(Through the year) Antiphon: The Virgin Mary is taken up into the heavenly chamber, where the King of Kings sits on his throne, brilliant with stars.

(In Advent) Antiphon: Hail Mary, full of grace, the Lord is

with thee: blessed art thou amongst women.

(Christmas time) Antiphon: When thou was born after an ineffable manner, the Scriptures were then fulfilled; thou didst descend like rain upon a fleece, to save mankind: O our God, we give thee praise.

Psalm 100: Jubilate Deo.

Sing joyfully to the Lord, ye people of the earth: serve the Lord with delight of heart. Present yourselves before him in transports of holy joy. Know ye, that the Lord himself is the only God: he hath made us, and not we ourselves. We are his people, and the sheep of his pasture: enter into the porches of his temple, singing his divine praises, and giving him glory. Praise ye his name: for the Lord is sweet; his mercies are eternal, and his truth endureth from generation to generation.

Glory be to the Father, and to the Son, and to the Holy Ghost. As it was in the beginning, is now, and ever shall be, world without end. Amen.

(Through the year) Antiphon: The Virgin Mary is taken up into the heavenly chamber, where the King of kings sits on his throne, brilliant with stars.

(In Advent) Antiphon: Hail Mary, full of grace, the Lord is with thee: blessed art thou amongst women.

(Christmas time) Antiphon: When thou wast born after an ineffable manner, the Scriptures were then fulfilled; thou didst descend like rain upon a fleece, to save mankind: O our God, we give thee praise.

* * * * * * * * *

(Through the year) Antiphon: We run after the odor of thy perfumes: the young virgins have exceedingly loved thee.

(In Advent) Antiphon: Do not fear, Mary, thou hast found grace with the Lord; behold, thou shalt conceive and bring forth a Son.

(Christmas time) Antiphon: In the bush, which Moses saw burning without consuming, we acknowledge the preservation of thy admirable virginity: O mother of God, make intercession for us.

Psalm 63: *Deus, Deus Meus.*

O God, my God, I watch unto thee from the dawn of the day. My soul hath thirsted after thee; oh, by how many titles doth my whole being belong to thee! In this desert, uncultivated, and barren land, I shall be in thy presence, if I were in the sanctuary, to contemplate thy power and thy glory.

For thy mercies are preferable to many lives: my lips shall not cease to praise thee. Thus I will bless thee all my life: and I will lift up my hands to praise thy name. May my soul be replenished with thy benedictions, as with the fatness of marrow: and my mouth shall praise thee with rapturous joy.

I have called thee to mind on my bed at night, and in the morning I will meditate on thee; because thou hast been my helper. Under the cover of thy wings I will rejoice; my soul is attached to thee: thy right hand hath protected me. And my enemies have in vain sought my soul; they shall descend into the lower regions of the earth: unto the justice of the sword they shall be delivered, and shall become a prey to ravenous foxes. But the king shall rejoice in God: all, who swear by Him shall be glorified; because he hath stopped the mouths of those who speak evil things.

The Gloria Patri is not said here.

* * * * * * * * * *

Psalm 67: Deus Misereatur Nostri

May God have mercy on us, and bless us: may he regard us with a favorable countenance, and have mercy on us. May we know Thy ways on earth, and may all nations seek thy salvation. May the people confess thee, O God: may all present to thee their praises.

Let the nations be glad, and rejoice: for thou dost judge the people with equity, and rulest over all the nations of the earth. May the people confess thee, O God: may all present to thee their praises: the earth hath yielded forth her fruit. May the Lord, our God, bless us, may he give us his blessing: and may all the bounds of the earth fear him.

Glory be to the Father, and to the Son, and to the Holy Ghost. As it was in the beginning, is now, and ever shall be, world without end. Amen.

(Through the year) Antiphon: We run after the odor of thy perfumes: the young virgins have exceedingly loved thee.

(In Advent) Antiphon: Do not fear, Mary, thou hast found grace with the Lord; behold, thou shalt conceive and bring forth a Son.

(Christmas time) Antiphon: In the bush, which Moses saw burning without consuming, we acknowledge the preservation of thy admirable virginity: O Mother of God, make intercession for us.

(Through the year) Antiphon: Thou art blessed by the Lord, O daughter, for through thee we have been made partakers of the fruit of life.

(In Advent) Antiphon: The Lord will give him the throne of David, his father, and he shall reign forever.

(Christmas time) Antiphon: The root of Jesse hath budded forth: a star hath arisen out of Jacob: a virgin hath brought forth the Savior: we give thee praise, O our God.

Daniel 3: Canticle of the three Children.

All ye works of the Lord, bless the Lord: praise and extol him forever.
Bless the Lord, ye angels of the Lord: ye heavens bless the Lord.
All ye waters, which lie suspended on the firmament, bless the Lord: bless the Lord, all ye powers of the Lord.
Sun and moon, bless the Lord: stars of the firmament, bless the Lord.
Every shower and dew, bless the Lord: all ye tempestuous winds, bless the Lord.
Fire and heat, bless the Lord: cold and heat, bless the Lord.
Dews and hoar-frosts, bless the Lord: frost and cold, bless the Lord.
Ice and snow, bless the Lord: nights and days, bless the Lord.
Light and darkness, bless the Lord: lightnings and clouds, bless the Lord.
May the earth bless the Lord; may it praise and extol him forever.
Mountains and hills, bless the Lord: herbs and plants, bless the Lord.
Ye fountains, bless the Lord: seas and rivers, bless the Lord.
Whales, and all ye creatures which live in the waters, bless the

Lord: all ye birds of the air, bless the Lord.

All beasts and cattle, bless the Lord: ye children of men, bless the Lord.

May Israel bless the Lord; may he praise and extol him forever.
Ye priests of the Lord, bless the Lord: ye servants of the Lord, bless the Lord.

Spirits and souls of the just, bless the Lord: ye holy and humble of heart, bless the Lord.

O Ananias, Azarias, Misael, bless ye the Lord: praise and extol him forever.

Let us bless the Father, and the Son, with the Holy Ghost; let us praise and glorify him forever.

Blessed art thou, O Lord, in the firmament of heaven: to thee be rendered all praise, honor, and glory, forever.

The Gloria Patri is not said here.

(Through the year) Antiphon: Thou art blessed by the Lord, O daughter, for through thee we have been made partakers of the fruit of life.

(In Advent) Antiphon: The Lord will give him the throne of David, his father, and he shall reign forever.

(Christmas time) Antiphon: The root of Jesse hath budded forth: a star hath arisen out of Jacob: a virgin hath brought forth the Savior: we give thee praise, O our God.

* * * * * * * * * *

(Through the year) Antiphon: Thou art fair and beautiful, O daughter of Jerusalem, formidable as an army in battle array.

(In Advent) Antiphon: Behold the handmaid of the Lord, be it done unto me according to thy word.

(Christmas time) Antiphon: Behold Mary hath borne to us the Savior, whom John seeing, cried out: Behold the Lamb of God, behold him, who taketh away the sins of the world, Alleluia.

Psalm 148: Laudate Dominum

Praise the Lord in the heavens: praise him in the highest places.

Praise him, all ye his angels: praise him, ye celestial powers.

Praise him, sun and moon; praise him, all ye stars and light.

Praise him, O heaven of heavens, and may the waters that are over the firmament praise the name of the Lord.

For he hath spoken the word, and all things were made: he hath commanded, and they were created.

He hath established his works for length of ages: he prescribed to them his wise regulations, which shall not be transgressed.

Praise the Lord, from the earth, ye dragons and all ye depths.

Fire, hail, snow, ice, and stormy winds which obey his orders: Mountains and all hills: fruit-bearing trees, and all cedars.

Beasts, and herds of cattle: reptiles and birds of the air: Kings of the earth, and all ye people: princes, and judges of the earth.

Young men and maidens: the old with the young, let them praise the name of the Lord: for his name alone is most worthy of all praise.

His praise is above heaven and earth, and he hath exalted the power of his people.

May hymns of praise be rendered to him by all his saints: by the children of Israel, his cherished people.

The Gloria Patri is not said here.

* * * * * * * * * *

Psalm 149: Cantate Domine

Sing to the Lord a new canticle: may his praises resound in

the assembly of the Saints. May Israel rejoice in the God, who made him: may the sons of Sion exult in their king.

May they celebrate his name in choir: and honor him by concert on the timbrel and the psaltery. For the Lord is well pleased with his people, and he will exalt the meek unto salvation. The Saints in glory shall be filled with joy: they shall rejoice on their couches.

Sublime praises of God are in their mouths; and two-edged swords in their hands, to execute vengeance on the nations, and chastisement on the people; to bind their kings in fetters, and their nobles with iron manacles. They shall thus exercise the decreed justice: this glory is reserved for all his saints.

The Gloria Patris is not said here.

Psalm 150: Laudate Dominum

Praise the Lord in his sanctuary: praise him in the firmament of his power.

Praise him in his mighty deeds: praise him according to his exceeding greatness.

Praise him with the sound of the trumpet: praise him on the psaltery and the harp.

Praise him on the timbrel and in choir: praise him on stringed instruments, and on the organ.

Praise him with the best sounding cymbals, praise him on instruments of jubilee: may every living creature praise the Lord.

Glory be to the Father, and to the Son, and to the Holy Ghost. As it was in the beginning, is now, and ever shall be, world without end. Amen.

(Through the year) Antiphon: Thou art fair and beautiful, O daughter of Jerusalem, formidable as an army in battle array.

(In Advent) Antiphon: Behold the handmaid of the Lord, be it done unto me according to thy word.

(Christmas time) Antiphon: Behold Mary hath borne to us the Savior, whom John seeing cried out: Behold the Lamb of God, behold him, who taketh away the sins of the world, alleluia.

* * * * * * * * * *

The Little Chapter through the year except in Advent

Canticle of Canticles 6:9

The daughters of Sion beheld her, and declared her most blessed, and queens have highly praised her.

R. Thanks be to God.

In Advent

Isaiah 11:1

There shall spring forth a branch out of the root of Jesse, and a flower shall arise out of its stock; and the Spirit of the Lord shall rest upon him.

R. Thanks be to God.

Hymn

O Mary! Whilst thy Maker blest
Is nourished at thy virgin breast,
Such glory shines, that stars, though bright,
Compared to thee, all lose their light.

The loss that man in Eve deplores,
Thy fruitful womb in Christ restores,

And makes the way to heaven free
For those who mourning follow thee.

By thee the heavenly gates display,
And show the light of endless day,
Sing, ransomed nations, sing and own
Your ransom was a Virgin's Son.

To thee O Jesus, God's own Son,
Be everlasting homage done,
To God the Father, we repeat
The same, and to the Paraclete. Amen.

V. Blessed art thou among women.

R. And blessed is the fruit of thy womb.

* * * * * * * * * *

(Through the year) Antiphon: O blessed Mary, Mother of God, and ever virgin, temple of the Lord, and sanctuary of the Holy Ghost, thou alone didst please our Lord Jesus Christ, in a most singular and perfect manner: pray for the people, plead for the clergy, and intercede for the devout.

(In Easter time) Antiphon: O Queen of heaven, rejoice, Alleluia, because He, whom thou didst deserve to bear, alleluia, is risen again, as He foretold, alleluia: pray for us to God, alleluia.

(In Advent) Antiphon: The Holy Ghost shall come upon thee, Mary: do not fear, thou shalt have in thy womb the Son of God, alleluia.

(Christmas time) Antiphon: A most sublime mystery is made manifest on this day: wonders are wrought in nature; God is made man, still remaining what he was; he assumed what he was not; he suffered no mixture, nor division.

The Canticle of Zachariah. Luke 1:68-79

Blessed be the Lord, the God of Israel: because he hath visited and effected the redemption of his people. And hath raised up a powerful Savior for us, in the house of David, his servant.

As he promised by the mouth of his holy prophets, from the beginning: To save us from our enemies, and from the hands of all who hate us: To communicate his mercy to us, as well as to our fathers; and to recall to mind the holy covenant made to them.

The oath, which he hath sworn to our father Abraham, that he would grant us the grace.
That, being rescued from the fear and power of our enemies, we may serve him in holiness and righteousness in his presence, all the days of our lives.

And thou, O happy child, shalt be called the prophet of the Most High: for thou shalt go before the face of the Lord to prepare his ways: To give his people the knowledge of salvation unto the remission of their sins.

Through the bowels of the mercy of our God: with which he, like the rising sun from on high, hath visited us. To give light to those, who sit in darkness and in the shade of death: to guide our feet into the ways of peace.

Glory be to the Father, and to the Son, and to the Holy Ghost. As it was in the beginning, is now, and ever shall be, world without end. Amen.

* * * * * * * * *

(Through the year) Antiphon: O blessed Mary, mother of God, and ever virgin, temple of the Lord, and sanctuary of the Holy Ghost, thou alone didst please our Lord Jesus Christ, in a most singular and perfect manner: pray for the people, plead for the clergy, and intercede for the devout.

(In Easter time) Antiphon: O Queen of heaven, rejoice, Alleluia, because He, whom thou didst deserve to bear, alleluia, is risen again, as He foretold, alleluia: pray for us to God, alleluia.

(In Advent) Antiphon: The Holy Ghost shall come upon thee, Mary: do not fear, thou shalt have in thy womb the Son of God, alleluia.

(Christmas time) Antiphon: A most sublime mystery is made manifest on this day: wonders are wrought in nature; God is made man, still remaining what he was; he assumed what he was not; he suffered no mixture, nor division.

Lord, have mercy on us,
Christ, have mercy on us,
Lord, have mercy on us.

V. O Lord, hear my prayer.
R. And let my cry come unto thee.

Or, if the president be a priest or a deacon:

V. The Lord be with you.
R. And with thy Spirit.

Let us pray.

The prayer through the year, except at Christmas time.

O God, who was pleased that thy eternal Word, when the angel delivered his message, should take flesh in the womb of the blessed Virgin Mary: give ear to our humble petitions, and grant that we, who believe her to be truly the Mother of God, may be assisted by her prayers, through the same Christ our Lord. Amen.

At Christmas time

O God, who, by the fruitful virginity of blessed Mary, has given to mankind the rewards of eternal salvation, grant, we beseech thee, that we may experience her intercession for us, by whom we deserved to receive the author of life, our Lord Jesus Christ thy Son.

R. Amen.

Commemoration of the Saints

(Through the year, except in Advent)

Antiphon: All ye saints of God, vouchsafe to make intercession for the salvation of us, and of all mankind.

V. Rejoice in the Lord, ye just, and be exceedingly glad.

R. And exult in glory, all ye upright of heart.

Let us pray.

Protect, O Lord, thy people, and grant us thy continual assistance, which we humbly beg with confidence, through the intercession of St. Peter and St. Paul, and of thy other apostles. May all the saints, we beseech thee, O Lord, always assist our weakness, that whilst we celebrate their merits we may experience their protection; grant us thy peace in our days, and banish all evils from thy Church: prosperously guide the steps, actions, and desires of us, and of all thy servants, in the way of salvation: give eternal blessings to our benefactors, and grant everlasting rest to all the faithful departed.   Through our Lord Jesus Christ, thy son, who liveth and reigneth with thee and the Holy Ghost, one God, world without end.

R. Amen.

Commemoration of the Saints in Advent

Antiphon: Behold, the Lord will come, and all his saints with him: and there shall be a great light on that day, alleluia.

V. Behold, the Lord shall appear on a bright cloud.

R. And with him thousands of saints.

Let us pray.

Visit and purify our consciences, O God, that Jesus Christ, thy Son, our Lord, coming with all his Saints, may find in us an abode prepared for his reception: who liveth and reigneth with thee and the Holy Ghost, one God, world without end.

R. Amen.

After the Commemoration of the Saints, the following Versicles are said.

V. O Lord, hear my prayer.
R. And let my cry come unto thee.

V. Let us bless the Lord.

R. Thanks be to God.

V. May the souls of the faithful departed, through the mercy of God, rest in peace.
R. Amen.

(In silence) Our Father, etc.

V. May the Lord grant us his peace.
R. And life everlasting. Amen.

Then is recited one of the Antiphons of the Blessed Virgin Mary, according to the time of the year, as in Appendix I.

PRIME

Recited at 6 a.m.

O divine and adorable Lord Jesus Christ, who has graciously redeemed us by thy bitter passion and death, we offer up this hour of Prime to thy honor and glory, and most humbly beseech thee, through the great humility thou didst undergo, in being convicted before the false tribunals of Pilate and Herod, where thou was reviled by the soldiery, clothed like a fool, and degraded below the worst of criminals, to grant us true humility of heart, and sincere sentiments of our own wretchedness, misery, poverty, blindness, and destitution, that we may never esteem ourselves above the lowest of our fellow-creatures, but always acknowledge ourselves truly the worst of sinners, so that our extreme misery may excite thy tender compassion and infinite goodness to forgive us all our sins, to replenish us with thy divine grace here, and to elevate us to eternal glory in heaven. Amen.

Hail, Mary, full of grace, the Lord is with thee. Blessed art thou amongst women, and blessed is the fruit of thy womb, Jesus. Holy Mary, Mother of God, pray for us sinners, now, and in the hour of our death. Amen.

V. Incline unto my aid, O God.
R. O Lord, make haste to help me.

Glory be to the Father, and to the Son, and to the Holy Ghost. As it was in the beginning, is now, and ever shall be, world without end. Amen, Alleluia.

During Lent: *Praise be to thee, O Lord, king of eternal glory.*

Hymn

Remember thou, Creator Lord,
The Father God's co-equal Word,
To save mankind, from virgin's womb
Our human nature didst assume.

O happy Mary, full of grace,
Dear mother of the Prince of Peace,
Protect us from our evil foe,
And bliss at death on us bestow.

To thee, O Jesus, Mary's Son,
Be everlasting homage done,
To God the Father we repeat
The same, and to the Paraclete. Amen.

* * * * * * * * * *

(Through the year) Ant. Mary is taken up into heaven: the angels rejoice, and with praises bless the Lord.

(In Advent) Ant. The angel Gabriel was sent to the Virgin Mary, espoused to Joseph.

(Christmas time) Ant. O admirable intercourse! The Creator of mankind, assuming a body animated with a soul, was pleased to be born of a virgin, and becoming man without human concurrence, made us partakers of his divine nature.

Psalm 54: Deus In Nomine Tuo.

Save me, O God, in thy name: and in thy power do me justice. O God, graciously hear my prayer: give ear to my words. For strangers have risen up against me, and the strong ones have sought to take away my soul: and they have not been mindful of the presence of God. For behold, God is my helper: and the Lord is the protector of my soul.

Turn back on my enemies the evils which they wish to do to me: and destroy them according to the truth of thy words. I will freely sacrifice to thee and will praise thy holy name, O Lord: because it is just: For thou hast rescued me from all trouble: and I have regarded my enemies without fear.

Glory be to the Father, and to the Son, and to the Holy Ghost. As it was in the beginning, is now, and ever shall be, world without end. Amen, Alleluia.

* * * * * * * * * *

Psalm 85: Benedixisti Domine.

O Lord, thou hast blessed thy land: thou hast set free the captives of Jacob. Thou hast forgiven the iniquity of thy people: thou hast pardoned all their sins. Thou hast mitigated all thine anger: and withdrawn from us thy indignation.

Convert us to thee, O God, our Savior: and turn away thy wrath from us. Wilt thou be forever angry with us? Or wilt thou continue thy wrath from generation to generation? O God, thou wilt cheer us with thy reconciliation: and thy people shall rejoice in thee.

Show us, O Lord, thy mercy, and grant us thy salvation. I will hear what the Lord God will speak to me: for he will speak peace unto his people.
He will announce it to his Saints, and to those whose heart is truly converted to him. Surely his salvation is near to those who fear him: that his glory may dwell among us.

Mercy and truth have met each other: justice and peace have

kissed.

Truth is sprung out of the earth, and justice hath regarded us from the height of heaven. For the Lord will communicate his goodness: and the earth shall yield her fruit. Justice shall proceed before him: and shall direct his steps in the true path.

Glory be to the Father, and to the Son, and to the Holy Ghost. As it was in the beginning, is now, and ever shall be, world without end. Amen, Alleluia.

* * * * * * * * * *

Psalm 116: Laudate Dominum

Praise the Lord, all ye nations: praise him, all ye people. For his mercy is confirmed upon us: and the truth of the Lord remaineth forever.

Glory be to the Father, and to the Son, and to the Holy Ghost. As it was in the beginning, is now, and ever shall be, world without end. Amen, Alleluia.

(Through the year) Ant. Mary is taken up into heaven: the angels rejoice, and with praises bless the Lord.

(In Advent) Ant. The angel Gabriel was sent to the Virgin Mary, espoused to Joseph.

(Christmas time) Ant. O admirable intercourse! The Creator of mankind, assuming a body animated with a soul, was pleased to be born of a virgin, and becoming man without human concurrence, made us partakers of his divine nature.

The Little Chapter through the year, except in Advent

Little Chapter. Canticle of Canticles 6:10

Who is she, that cometh forth as the morning rising, beautiful like the moon, bright as the sun, formidable as an army in battle array?

R. Thanks be to God.

The Little Chapter in Advent

Little Chapter. Isaiah 7:14-15

Behold, a virgin shall conceive, and bring forth a son, and his name shall be called Emmanuel. He shall eat butter and honey, that he may know how to reject evil, and choose good.

R. Thanks be to God.

V. Vouchsafe, O sacred Virgin, to accept my praises.
R. Give me strength against thy enemies.

Lord, have mercy on us.
Christ, have mercy on us.
Lord, have mercy on us.

V. O Lord, hear my prayer.
R. And let my cry come unto thee.

Let us pray.

(Through the year) O God, who was pleased to make choice of the chaste womb of the blessed Virgin Mary for thy abode; grant, we beseech thee, that, being protected by the assistance

of her intercession, we may celebrate her memory with spiritual joy: Who livest and reignest with the Father and the Holy Ghost, one God, world without end.
R. Amen.

(In Advent) O God, who was pleased that thy eternal Word, when the angel delivered his message, should take flesh in the womb of the blessed Virgin Mary, give ear to our humble petitions, and grant that we, who believe her to be truly the mother of God, may be assisted by her prayers. Through the same Lord Jesus Christ thy Son, who liveth and reigneth with thee and the Holy Ghost, one God, world without end.
R. Amen.

(Christmas time) O God, who, by the fruitful virginity of blessed Mary, has given to mankind the rewards of eternal salvation, grant, we beseech thee, that we may experience her intercession, by whom we have received the author of life, our Lord Jesus Christ, thy Son: Who liveth and reigneth with thee and the Holy Ghost, one God, world without end.
R. Amen.

V. O Lord, hear my prayer.
R. And let my cry come unto thee.

V. Let us bless the Lord.
R. Thanks be to God.

V. May the souls of the faithful departed, through the mercy of God, rest in peace.
R. Amen.

TERCE

Recited at 9 a.m.

O divine and adorable Lord, Jesus Christ, who has graciously redeemed us by thy bitter passion and death, we offer up this hour of Terce to thy honor and glory: and most humbly beseech thee, through the torments thou didst endure in being cruelly scourged at a pillar, crowned with thorns, and unjustly condemned to be crucified, to grant us patience and longanimity under the scourges of temporal afflictions, courage to walk in the thorny road to the narrow gate, which opens to bliss, and perseverance under all the crosses of this life, which are the portion of the elect, that by suffering for our sins we may fully satisfy thy divine justice on earth, and may enter into thy glory immediately after death. Amen.

Hail, Mary, full of grace, the Lord is with thee. Blessed art thou among women, and blessed is the fruit of thy womb, Jesus. Holy Mary, Mother of God, pray for us sinners, now, and in the hour of our death. Amen.

V. Incline unto my aid, O God.
R. O Lord, make haste to help me.

Glory be to the Father, and to the Son, and to the Holy Ghost. As it was in the beginning, is now, and ever shall be, world without end. Amen, Alleluia.

During Lent: *Praise be to thee, O Lord, king of eternal glory.*

Hymn

Remember thou, Creator Lord,
The Father God's co-equal Word,
To save mankind, from Virgin's womb
Our human nature didst assume.

O happy Mary, full of grace,
Dear mother of the Prince of Peace,
Protect us from our evil foe,
And bliss at death on us bestow.

To thee, O Jesus, Mary's Son,
Be everlasting homage done,
To God the Father we repeat
The same, and to the Paraclete.
Amen.

(Through the year) Ant. The Virgin Mary is taken up into the heavenly chamber where the King of kings sits on his starry throne.

(In Advent) Ant. Hail, Mary, full of grace, the Lord is with thee; blessed art thou among women.

(Christmas time) Ant. When thou was born after an ineffable manner, the Scriptures were then fulfilled: thou didst descend like rain upon a fleece, to save mankind: O our God, we give thee praise.

Psalm 120: Ad Dominum

I cried out to the Lord in my extreme distress, and he graciously heard me. O Lord, deliver my soul from unjust lips and from a deceitful tongue. What shall be done to thee, or what punishment shalt thou receive for thy deceitful tongue? Thou shalt feel the sharp arrows of the Almighty, accompanied with destructive burning coals.

How miserable I am, that my exile is so prolonged! I dwell here among the inhabitants of Cedar: my soul hath been long a sojourner. I was peaceable with those who hated peace: when I spoke to them, they opposed me without any cause.

Glory be to the Father, and to the Son, and to the Holy Ghost. As it was in the beginning, is now, and ever shall be, world without end. Amen, Alleluia.

* * * * * * * *

Psalm 121: Levavi Oculos.

I lifted up my eyes toward the mountains: from whence I expect assistance. My help is from the Lord, who made heaven and earth. May he not suffer thy foot to be moved: neither may he slumber, who is thy guardian. Behold, he shall neither slumber nor sleep, that keepeth Israel.

The Lord watcheth over thee, the Lord is thy protector; he is at thy right hand. The sun shall not burn thee by day, nor shall the moon molest thee by night. The Lord preserveth thee from all evil: may the Lord still protect thy soul. May the Lord watch over thee coming in and going out, now and forevermore.

Glory be to the Father, and to the Son, and to the Holy Ghost. As it was in the beginning, is now, and ever shall be, world without end. Amen, Alleluia.

Psalm 122: Laetatus Sum

I rejoiced in what hath been told me: we are to go up to the house of the Lord. Our feet have stood in thy courts, O Jerusalem. Jerusalem, which is now building like a city, all whose parts are well combined.
For thither the tribes went up, the tribes of the Lord; according to the ordinances given to Israel, to praise the name of the Lord. For there were placed the judgment-seats, the judgment-seats over the house of David.

Pray for whatever maketh for the peace of Jerusalem; and may plenty be to all who love thee.

May peace be in thy strength and plenty within thy walls. For the sake of my brethren and of all my neighbors, I have advocated thy peace. For the sake of the house of the Lord our God, I have sought good things for thee.

Glory be to the Father, and to the Son, and to the Holy Ghost. As it was in the beginning, is now, and ever shall be, world without end. Amen, Alleluia.

(Through the year) Ant. The Virgin Mary is taken up into the heavenly chamber where the King of kings sits on his starry throne.

(In Advent) Ant. Hail, Mary, full of grace, the Lord is with thee; blessed art thou among women.

(Christmas time) Ant. When thou was born after an ineffable manner, the Scriptures were then fulfilled: thou didst descend like rain upon a fleece, to save mankind: O our God, we give thee praise.

Terce

Little Chapter through the year, except in Advent.

Little Chapter. Ecclesiasticus 24:15

And so was I established in Sion, and in the holy city likewise I rested, and my power was in Jerusalem.

R. Thanks be to God.

The Little Chapter in Advent

Little Chapter. Isaiah 11:1-2

There shall spring forth a branch out of the root of Jesse, and a flower shall arise out of its stock: and the Spirit of the Lord shall rest upon Him.

R. Thanks be to God.

V. Grace is spread on thy lips.
R. Therefore God hath blessed thee forever.

Lord, have mercy on us.
Christ, have mercy on us.
Lord, have mercy on us.

V. O Lord, hear my prayer.
R. And let my cry come unto thee.

The Prayer through the year, except in Advent

O God, who by the fruitful virginity of blessed Mary, has given to mankind the rewards of eternal salvation; grant, we beseech thee, that we may experience her intercession for us, by whom we deserved to receive the author of life, our Lord Jesus Christ thy Son, who liveth and reigneth with thee and

63

the Holy Ghost, one God, world without end. Amen.

Let us pray.

The Prayer in Advent

O God, who was pleased that thy eternal Word, when the angel delivered his message, should take flesh in the womb of the blessed Virgin Mary; give ear to our humble petitions, and grant that we, who believe her to be truly the Mother of God, may be helped by her prayers. Through the same Lord, Jesus Christ, who liveth and reigneth with thee and the Holy Ghost, one God, world without end. Amen.

V. O Lord, hear my prayer.
R. And let my cry come unto thee.

V. Let us bless the Lord.
R. Thanks be to God.

V. May the souls of the faithful departed, through the mercy of God, rest in peace.
R. Amen.

SEXT

O divine and adorable Lord, Jesus Christ, who has graciously redeemed us by thy bitter passion and death, we offer up this hour of Sext to thy honor and glory; and most humbly beseech thee, through the fainting thou didst experience in bearing the cross from Pilate's tribunal to Calvary, and the excessive pains thou didst suffer when thy tender hands and feet were cruelly pierced through with gross nails, and fastened to the cross, to grant us thy strengthening grace to arise immediately whenever we fall into sin, and to restrain our hands, our feet, and our other sensitive powers from injuring our neighbor, and from evil deeds, that we may rise up, and go to our celestial Father with our hands replete with good works, to merit thy eternal rewards. Amen.

Hail, Mary, full of grace, the Lord is with thee. Blessed art thou among women, and blessed is the fruit of thy womb, Jesus. Holy Mary, Mother of God, pray for us sinners, now, and in the hour of our death. Amen.

V. Incline unto my aid, O God.

R. O Lord, make haste to help me.

Glory be to the Father, and to the Son, and to the Holy Ghost. As it was in the beginning, is now, and ever shall be, world without end. Amen, Alleluia.

During Lent: *Praise be to thee, O Lord, king of eternal glory.*

Hymn

Remember thou, Creator Lord,
The Father God's co-equal Word,
To save mankind, from Virgin's womb
Our human nature didst assume.

O happy Mary, full of grace,
Dear mother of the Prince of Peace,
Protect us from our evil foe,
And bliss at death on us bestow.

To thee, O Jesus, Mary's Son,
Be everlasting homage done,
To God the Father we repeat
The same, and to the Paraclete. Amen.

(Through the year) Ant. We run after the odor of thy perfumes:
the young virgins have exceedingly loved thee.

(In Advent) Ant. Fear not, Mary, thou hast found grace with
the Lord: behold, thou shalt conceive, and bring forth a son.

(Christmas time) Ant. In the bush, which Moses saw burn
without consuming, we acknowledge the preservation of thy
admirable virginity: O Mother of God, make intercession for
us.

Psalm 123: Ad Te Levavi.

To thee have I lifted up my eyes, who dwellest in heaven.
Behold, as the eyes of servants look to the bountiful hands of
their masters. And as the eyes of the handmaid look to the
bountiful hands of her mistress: so are our eyes fixed on the
Lord, our God, until he have mercy upon us.

Have mercy on us, O Lord, have mercy on us; for we are overwhelmed with humiliation: For our soul is deeply afflicted, being an object of reproach to the rich, and of contempt to the proud.

Glory be to the Father, and to the Son, and to the Holy Ghost. As it was in the beginning, is now, and ever shall be, world without end. Amen, Alleluia.

* * * * * * * * * *

Psalm 124: *Nisi Quia Dominus*

If it had not been that the Lord was with us, let Israel now say: If it had not been that the Lord was with us, when men rose up against us, perhaps they had engulfed us alive: When their fury raged against us, they would have probably overpowered us, like a raging wave, and sunk us.

Our soul has waded across the torrent: perhaps our soul has passed through waves of the most intolerable evils. Blessed be the Lord, who has not delivered us a prey to be torn by their teeth.

Our soul has been saved, like a sparrow which escapes the snare of the fowlers. The snare has been broken, and we are delivered. Our help is in the name of the Lord, who made heaven and earth.

Glory be to the Father, and to the Son, and to the Holy Ghost. As it was in the beginning, is now, and ever shall be, world without end. Amen, Alleluia.

Psalm 125: *Qui Confidunt.*

They who trust in the Lord shall be as mount Sion: he who dwelleth in Jerusalem shall never be disturbed. Mountains encompass it on every side, the Lord doth protect his people, now, and forevermore. Because the Lord will not permit the chastisement of sinners to fall on the righteous: lest the just are induced to stain their hands with iniquity.

Be kind, O Lord, to those who are good, and to the upright of heart. But such as are inclined to deceive and to ensnare; the Lord shall number among the workers of iniquity: peace upon Israel.

Glory be to the Father, and to the Son, and to the Holy Ghost. As it was in the beginning, is now, and ever shall be, world without end. Amen, Alleluia.

(Through the year) Ant. We run after the odor of thy perfumes: the young virgins have exceedingly loved thee.

(In Advent) Ant. Fear not, Mary, thou hast found grace with the Lord: behold, thou shalt conceive, and bring forth a son.

(Christmas time) Ant. In the bush, which Moses saw burn without consuming, we acknowledge the preservation of thy admirable virginity: O Mother of God, make intercession for us.

Little Chapter through the year, except in Advent.

Ecclesticus 24:16

I settled myself among a people whom the Lord hath honored, and hath chosen for his portion and inheritance, and I have fixed my abode in the company of all the Saints.

R. Thanks be to God.

The Little Chapter In Advent

Luke 1:32-33

The Lord God will give him the throne of his Father David, and he will eternally reign over the house of Jacob, and his kingdom shall never end.

R. Thanks be to God.

V. Blessed art thou among women.
R. And blessed is the fruit of thy womb.

Lord, have mercy on us.
Christ, have mercy on us.
Lord, have mercy on us.

V. O Lord, hear my prayer.
R. And let my cry come unto thee.

Let us pray.

(Through the year) Grant us, O merciful God, strength against all weakness; that we, who celebrate the memory of the holy Mother of God, may by the help of her intercession rise again from our iniquities. Through the same Lord Jesus Christ thy Son, who liveth and reigneth with thee and the Holy Ghost, one God, world without end.
R. Amen.

(In Advent) O God, who was pleased that thy eternal Word, when the angel delivered his message, should take flesh in the womb of the blessed Virgin Mary, give ear to our humble

petitions, and grant, that we who believe her to be truly the mother of God, may be helped by her prayers. Through the same Lord Jesus Christ, thy Son, who liveth and reigneth with thee and the Holy Ghost, one God, world without end.
R. Amen.

(Christmas time) O God, who, by the fruitful virginity of blessed Mary, has given to mankind the rewards of eternal salvation: grant, we beseech thee, that we may experience her intercession for us, by whom we deserved to receive the Author of life, our Lord Jesus Christ, thy Son, who liveth and reigneth with thee and the Holy Ghost, one God, world without end.
R. Amen.

V. O Lord, hear my prayer.
R. And let my cry come unto thee.

V. Let us bless the Lord.
R. Thanks be to God.

V. May the souls of the faithful departed, through the mercy of God, rest in peace.
R. Amen.

NONE

Recited at 3 p.m.

O divine and adorable Lord Jesus Christ, who has graciously redeemed us by thy bitter passion and death, we offer up this hour of None to thy honor and glory, and most humbly beseech thee, through the torments and agony thou didst suffer when hanging for three hours on the cross, and through thy precious death, which gave redemption and life to the world, and thy sacred burial, to grant us thy divine assistance, and the grace of the holy sacraments at our last hour and agony, and to give us a happy death, precious in thy sight, and pure from the least defilement of sin, that we may be at our death attended by thy holy angels, and by them borne up on high into those blissful regions, where we will contemplate thy divinity forevermore. Amen.

Hail, Mary, full of grace, the Lord is with thee. Blessed art thou among women, and blessed is the fruit of thy womb, Jesus. Holy Mary, mother of God, pray for us sinners, now, and in the hour of our death. Amen.

V. Incline unto my aid, O God.
R. O Lord, make haste to help me.

Glory be to the Father, and to the Son, and to the Holy Ghost. As it was in the beginning, is now, and ever shall be, world without end. Amen, Alleluia.

During Lent: *Praise be to thee, O Lord, king of eternal glory.*

71

Hymn

Remember thou, Creator Lord,
The Father God's co-equal Word,
To save mankind, from virgin's womb
Our human nature didst assume.

O happy Mary, full of Grace,
Dear mother of the Prince of Peace,
Protect us from our evil foe,
And bliss at death on us bestow.

To thee, O Jesus, Mary's Son,
Be everlasting homage done,
To God the Father we repeat
The same, and to the Paraclete. Amen.

(Through the year) Ant. Thou art fair and beautiful, O daughter of Jerusalem, formidable as an army in battle array.

(In Advent) Ant. Behold the handmaid of the Lord: be it done unto me according to thy word.

(Christmas time) Ant. Behold, Mary hath borne to us the Savior, whom John seeing, cried out: Behold the Lamb of God, behold him, who taketh away the sins of the world, alleluia.

Psalm 126: In Convertento.

When the Lord brings back the captives of Sion, we shall be like men cheered with comfort. Then shall our voices break forth in joyful praises, and our tongue in canticles of jubilee. Then shall they declare to their neighbors, that the Lord hath done great things for them.

The Lord hath done great things for us: we are therefore become joyful. Bring back, O Lord, our captive people, like a torrent in the south. They who sow in tears shall reap in joy. They went forth shedding tears, while they were sowing seeds. But they will return full of joy, bringing in the sheaves they have gathered.

Glory be to the Father, and to the Son, and to the Holy Ghost. As it was in the beginning, is now, and ever shall be, world without end. Amen, Alleluia.

* * * * * * * * * *

Psalm 127: *Nisi Dominus.*

Unless the Lord himself shall build up the house, they toil in vain who strive to build it. Unless the Lord shall guard the city, the sentinel doth watch in vain. It is useless for you to rise before the light: arise after you have taken rest, you who eat the bread of sorrow.

Since he will give sleep to his beloved ones: know that children are blessings from the Lord, and that a numerous offspring is also a reward. Like arrows in the hand of a powerful man, are the children of those, who have been reproved. Blessed is the man, whose desires are accomplished in them: he shall not be confounded, when he shall speak to his enemies before the courts.

Glory be to the Father, and to the Son, and to the Holy Ghost. As it was in the beginning, is now, and ever shall be, world without end. Amen, Alleluia.

Psalm 128: Beati Omnes.

Blessed are all who fear the Lord, who walk according to his ways. Because thou shalt partake of the labor of thy own hands: thou art happy, and replenished with all good things. Thy wife shall be like a fruitful vine, in a garden at the rear of thy house. Thy children, like young olive plants, all round thy table. Behold, thus shall the man be blessed, who feareth the Lord.

May the Lord bless thee from Sion: and mayest thou see the prosperity of Jerusalem all the days of thy life. And mayest thou see the sons of thy children, and peace given to Israel.

Glory be to the Father, and to the Son, and to the Holy Ghost. As it was in the beginning, is now, and ever shall be, world without end. Amen, Alleluia.

(Through the year) Ant. Thou art fair and beautiful, O daughter of Jerusalem, formidable as an army in battle array.

(In Advent) Ant. Behold the handmaid of the Lord: be it done unto me according to thy word.

(Christmas time) Ant. Behold, Mary hath borne to us the Savior, whom John seeing, cried out: Behold the Lamb of God, behold him, who taketh away the sins of the world, alleluia.

The Little Chapter through the year, except in Advent

Ecclesiasticus 24:20

I yielded forth a fragrant perfume in the streets, like cinnamon and aromatic balm: and, like the best myrrh, I spread around the sweetest odor.
R. Thanks be to God.

The Little Chapter In Advent

Isaiah 7:14

Behold, a virgin shall conceive, and bring forth a son, and his name shall be called Emmanuel. He shall eat butter and honey, that he may know how to reject evil, and choose the good.

R. Thanks be to God.

V. After childbirth thou didst remain a pure virgin.

R. O Mother of God, intercede for us.

Lord, have mercy on us.
Christ, have mercy on us.
Lord, have mercy on us.

V. O Lord, hear my prayer.
R. And let my cry come unto thee.

Let us pray.

(Through the year) Pardon, we beseech thee, O Lord, the sins of thy servants: that we, who are not able to please thee by our own actions, may be saved by the intercession of the mother of thy Son, our Lord: Who liveth and reigneth with thee and the Holy Ghost, one God, world without end.
R. Amen.

(In Advent) O God, who was pleased that thy eternal Word, when the angel delivered his message, should take flesh in the womb of the blessed Virgin Mary, give ear to our humble petitions, and grant that we who believe her to be truly the mother of God, may be helped by her prayers. Through the

same Lord Jesus Christ, thy Son, who liveth and reigneth with thee and the Holy Ghost, one God, world without end.
R. Amen.

(Christmas time) O God, who, by the fruitful virginity of blessed Mary, has given to mankind the rewards of eternal salvation: grant, we beseech thee, that we may experience her intercession for us, by whom we have received the Author of life, our Lord Jesus Christ, thy Son, who liveth and reigneth with thee and the Holy Ghost, one God, world without end.
R. Amen.

V. O Lord, hear my prayer.
R. And let my cry come unto thee.

V. Let us bless the Lord.
R. Thanks be to God.

V. May the souls of the faithful departed, through the mercy of God, rest in peace.
R. Amen.

VESPERS

Said at sundown

O divine and adorable Lord Jesus Christ, who has graciously redeemed us by thy bitter passion and death, we offer up these Vespers to thy honor and glory, and most humbly beseech thee, through thy dolorous agony and bloody sweat, which thou didst suffer in the garden, to grant us true contrition of heart, and sorrow for our sins, with a firm resolution never more to offend thee, but so satisfy thy divine justice for past iniquity. Amen.

Hail, Mary, full of grace, the Lord is with thee. Blessed art thou among women, and blessed is the fruit of thy womb, Jesus. Holy Mary, Mother of God, pray for us sinners, now, and in the hour of our death. Amen.

V. Incline unto my aid, O God.
R. O Lord, make haste to help me.

Glory be to the Father, and to the Son, and to the Holy Ghost. As it was in the beginning, is now, and ever shall be, world without end. Amen, Alleluia.

During Lent: *Praise be to thee, O Lord, king of eternal glory.*

(Through the year) Ant. While the king was on his couch, my perfumes sent forth an odor of sweetness.

(In Advent) Ant. The angel Gabriel was sent to the Virgin Mary, espoused to Joseph. Hail Mary, full of grace, the Lord is with thee. Blessed art thou amongst women. Alleluia.

(Christmas time) Ant. O admirable intercourse! The Creator of mankind, assuming a body animated with a soul, was pleased to be born of a Virgin; and becoming man without human concurrence, he made us partakers of his divine nature.

The Lord said to my Lord: Sit thou on my right hand. Until I make thy enemies thy footstool. The Lord shall send forth the scepter of thy power out of Sion: rule thou in the midst of thy enemies.

Thine shall be sovereignty in the day of thy might, in the brightness of the Saints: from the womb before the daystar I begot thee.

The Lord hath sworn, and he will not repent: Thou art a priest forever according to the order of Melchisedech. The Lord on thy right hand has subdued kings in the day of his wrath.

He shall judge the nations; he shall fill ruins: he shall crush heads in the land of many. Of the brook he shall drink in the way: therefore shall he raise up his head.

Glory be to the Father, and to the Son, and to the Holy Ghost: As it was in the beginning, is now, and ever shall be, world without end. Amen.

(Through the year) Ant. While the king was on his couch, my perfumes sent forth an odor of sweetness.

(In Advent) Ant. The angel Gabriel was sent to the Virgin Mary, espoused to Joseph.

(Christmas time) Ant. O admirable intercourse! The Creator of mankind, assuming a body animated with a soul, was pleased to be born of a Virgin; and becoming man without human concurrence, he made us partakers of his divine nature.

(Through the year) Ant. His left hand under my head, and his right hand shall embrace me.

(In Advent) Ant. Hail Mary, full of grace, the Lord is with thee. Blessed art thou amongst women. Alleluia.

(Christmas time) Ant. When thou wast born after an ineffable manner, the Scriptures were then fulfilled; thou didst descend like rain upon a fleece, to save mankind: O our God, we give thee praise.

Psalm 113: Laudate Pueri.

Praise the Lord, ye servants of the Lord: praise ye the name of the Lord. Let the name of the Lord be blessed, now and forevermore. From the rising of the sun to the setting thereof, worthy of praise is the name of the Lord.

High is the Lord above all nations: and above the heavens is his glory. Who is like unto the Lord our God, who dwelleth on high, and regardeth what is humble in heaven and on earth? Raising up the needy one from the earth, and from the dunghill lifting up the poor one, to place him with the princes, with the princes of his people. Who maketh the barren woman to dwell in her house, the joyful mother of many children.

Glory be to the Father, and to the Son, and to the Holy Ghost. As it was in the beginning, is now, and ever shall be, world without end. Amen, Alleluia.

(Through the year) Ant. His left hand under my head, and his right hand shall embrace me.

(In Advent) Ant. Hail Mary, full of grace, the Lord is with thee. Blessed art thou amongst women. Alleluia.

(Christmas time) Ant. When thou wast born after an ineffable manner, the Scriptures were then fulfilled; thou didst descend like rain upon a fleece, to save mankind: O our God, we give thee praise.

* * * * * * * * * *

(Through the year) Ant. I am black but beautiful, O ye daughters of Jerusalem: therefore hath the king loved me and brought me into his chamber.

(In Advent) Ant. Do not fear, Mary; thou hast found grace with the Lord: behold thou shalt conceive, and bring forth a Son.

(Christmas time) Ant. In the bush which Moses saw burn without consuming, we acknowledge the preservation of thy glorious virginity: O Mother of God, make intercession for us.

Psalm 122: Laetatus Sum In His.

I rejoiced in what hath been told me: We are to go up to the house of the Lord. Our feet have stood in thy courts, O Jerusalem, Jerusalem, which is now building like a city, all whose parts are joined together.

For thither the tribes went up, the tribes of the Lord; according to the ordinances given to Israel to praise the name of the Lord, for there were placed the judgment-seats, the judgment-seats over the house of David.

Ask for what tends to the peace of Jerusalem: and may plenty be to all who love thee. May peace be in thy strength; and plenty within thy walls. For the sake of my brethren and of my neighbors, I have advocated thy peace. For the sake of the house of the Lord, our God, I have sought good things for thee.

Glory be to the Father, and to the Son, and to the Holy Ghost. As it was in the beginning, is now, and ever shall be, world without end. Amen, Alleluia.

(Through the year) Ant. I am black but beautiful, O ye daughters of Jerusalem: therefore hath the king loved me, and brought me into his chamber.

(In Advent) Ant. Do not fear, Mary; thou hast found grace with the Lord: behold thou shalt conceive, and bring forth a Son.

(Christmas time) Ant. In the bush which Moses saw burn without consuming, we acknowledge the preservation of thy glorious virginity: O mother of God, make intercession for us.

* * * * * * * * * *

(Through the year) Ant. The winter is now past, the rain is over and gone: arise, my love and come.

(In Advent) Ant. The Lord will give him the throne of David, his father, and he shall reign forever.

(Christmas time) Ant. The root of Jesse hath budded forth: a star hath arisen out of Jacob: a Virgin hath brought forth the Savior: we give thee praise, O our God.

Psalm 127: Nisi Dominus.

Unless the Lord himself shall build up the house, in vain have labored the builders thereof; unless the Lord shall guard the city, in vain watcheth the sentinel thereof. It is in vain for you to rise before the light: arise after you have taken rest, you who eat the bread of sorrow, Since he will give sleep to his beloved ones:

Behold, children are an inheritance from the Lord, the fruit of the womb is a reward. Like arrows in the hand of a man of power, so shall be the children of those who have been rejected. Blessed is the man whose desire is filled with them; he shall not be confounded when he shall speak to his enemies at the gate.

Glory be to the Father, and to the Son, and to the Holy Ghost. As it was in the beginning, is now, and ever shall be, world without end. Amen, Alleluia.

(Through the year) Ant. The winter is now past, the rain is over and gone: arise, my love and come.

(In Advent) Ant. The Lord will give him the throne of David, his father, and he shall reign forever.

(Christmas time) Ant. The root of Jesse hath budded forth: a star hath arisen out of Jacob: a Virgin hath brought forth the Savior: we give thee praise, O our God.

* * * * * * * * * *

(Through the year) Ant. Thou art become beautiful and sweet in thy delights, O holy Mother of God.

(In Advent) Ant. Behold the handmaid of the Lord: be it done to me according to thy word.

(Christmas time) Ant. Behold, Mary hath borne us the Savior, whom John seeing, exclaimed: Behold the Lamb of God, behold him who taketh away the sins of the world, alleluia.

Psalm 147: Lauda Jerusalem.

O Jerusalem, praise the Lord: praise thy God, O Sion. For

strong hath he made the bolts of thy gates: he hath blessed thy children within thy walls. It is he who hath settled peace within thy borders: with the finest flour of wheat he feedeth thee. 'Tis he who sends forth his orders to the earth: his orders go with speed. 'Tis he who sendeth snow like flocks of wool: he sprinkleth his hoarfrost like ashes.

He sendeth down his hail like mouthfuls: who can stand the cold thereof? He will send forth his word, which shall melt it away: his spirit shall breathe, and the waters shall flow again. 'Tis he who maketh known his commandments to Jacob: his law and ordinances to Israel. He hath not done thus to every nation: nor hath he made known his law to them.

Glory be to the Father, and to the Son, and to the Holy Ghost. As it was in the beginning, is now, and ever shall be, world without end. Amen, Alleluia.

(Through the year) Ant. Thou art become beautiful and sweet in thy delights, O holy Mother of God.

(In Advent) Ant. Behold the handmaid of the Lord: be it done to me according to thy word.

(Christmas time) Ant. Behold, Mary hath borne us the Savior, whom John seeing, exclaimed: Behold the Lamb of God, behold him who taketh away the sins of the world, alleluia.

The Little Chapter through the year, except in Advent

Little Chapter. Ecclesiasticus 24:14

From the beginning, and before all ages, was I created, and I shall not cease to be in the world to come; and I have ministered before him in his holy abode.

R. Thanks be to God.

The Little Chapter In Advent

Little Chapter. Isaiah 11:1-2

There shall come forth a rod out of the root of Jesse, and a flower shall spring out of its root: and the Spirit of the Lord shall rest upon him.

R. Thanks be to God.

Kneel during the first four verses of the
Ave Maris Stella.

Hymn

Bright Mother of our Maker, hail,
Thou virgin ever blest;
The ocean's star, by which we sail,
And gain the port of rest.

While we this hail, addressed to thee,
From Gabriel's mouth rehearse,
Obtain that peace our lot may be,
And Eva's name reverse.
Release our long entangled mind
From all the snares of ill;
With heavenly light instruct the blind,
And all our vows fulfill.

Exert for us a mother's care,
And us thy children own:
Prevail with him to hear our prayer,
Who chose to be thy Son.

O spotless maid, whose virtues shine,
From all suspicion free,

Each action of our lives refine,
And make us pure like thee.

Preserve our lives unstained with ill
In this infected way,
That heaven alone our souls may fill
With joys that never decay.

To God the Father endless praise;
To God the Son the same,
And Holy Ghost, whose equal rays,
One equal glory claim. Amen.

V. Grace is spread on thy lips.
R. Therefore God hath blessed thee forever.

* * * * * * * * * *

(Through the year) Ant. O blessed Mother, and chaste virgin, glorious queen of the world, make intercession for us to the Lord.

(Easter time) Ant. O Queen of Heaven, rejoice, Alleluia, because He, whom thou didst deserve to bear, Alleluia, is risen again, as he foretold, Alleluia: pray for us to God, Alleluia.

(In Advent) Ant. The Holy Ghost shall come upon thee, Mary; do not fear, thou shalt have in thy womb the Son of God, Alleluia.

(Christmas time) Ant. Great is the mystery of our inheritance: the womb of a pure virgin became the temple of God: He who took flesh of her was not defiled: all nations shall come and say: glory be to thee, O Lord.

Magnificat: Luke 1:46.

My soul doth magnify the Lord. And my spirit hath rejoiced in God my Savior. Because he hath regarded the humility of his handmaid: behold from henceforth all generations shall call me blessed.

For he, who is mighty, hath done great things to me: and holy is his name. And his mercy is from generation to generation to them who fear him.

He hath shown might in his arm; he hath scattered the proud in the conceit of their heart. He hath cast down the mighty from their seats, and hath exalted the humble. He hath filled the hungry with good things, and the rich he hath sent away empty.

He hath received Israel his servant, being mindful of his mercy. As he spoke to our Fathers; to Abraham, and to his seed forever.

Glory be to the Father, and to the Son, and to the Holy Ghost. As it was in the beginning, is now, and ever shall be, world without end. Amen, Alleluia.

(Through the year) Ant. O blessed Mother, and chaste virgin, glorious queen of the world, make intercession for us to the Lord.

(Easter time) Ant. O Queen of Heaven, rejoice, Alleluia, because he, whom thou didst deserve to bear, Alleluia, is risen again, as he foretold, Alleluia: pray for us to God, Alleluia.

(In Advent) Ant. The Holy Ghost shall come upon thee, Mary; do not fear, thou shalt have in thy womb the Son of God, alleluia.

(Christmas time) Ant. Great is the mystery of our inheritance: the womb of a pure virgin became the temple of God: he, who took flesh of her, was not defiled: all nations shall come and say: glory be to thee, O Lord.

Lord, have mercy on us.
Christ, have mercy on us.
Lord, have mercy on us.

V. O Lord, hear my prayer.
R. And let my cry come unto thee.

If the president be a priest or deacon, instead of the last Versicle is always said the following: --observe this at each hour before and after the prayer.

V. The Lord be with you.
R. And with thy Spirit.

Let us pray.

(Through the year) Grant, we beseech thee, O Lord God, that we, thy servants, may enjoy constant health of mind and body; and by the glorious intercession of the ever blessed Virgin Mary, may be delivered from all temporal afflictions, and enjoy eternal bliss. Through Christ, our Lord.
R. Amen.

(In Advent) O God, who was pleased that thy eternal word, when the angel delivered his message, should take flesh in the womb of the blessed Virgin Mary; give ear to our humble petitions, and grant that we, who believe her to be truly the mother of God, may be assisted by her prayers. Through the same Christ our Lord.
R. Amen.

(Christmas time) O God, who by the fruitful virginity of the Blessed Virgin Mary, has given to mankind the rewards of eternal salvation; grant, we beseech thee, that we may experience her intercession, by whom we have received the author of life, our Lord Jesus Christ thy Son.
R. Amen.

Commemoration of the Saints

(Through the year, except Advent.)

Ant. All ye saints of God, vouchsafe to make intercession for the salvation of us and of all mankind.

V. Rejoice in the Lord, ye just and be exceedingly glad.

R. And exult in glory, all ye upright of heart.

Let us pray.

Protect, O Lord, thy people, and grant us thy continual assistance, which we humbly beg with confidence, through the intercession of St. Peter and St. Paul, and of thy other apostles. May all thy Saints, we beseech thee, O Lord, always assist our weakness, that whilst we celebrate their merits, we may experience their protection; grant us thy peace in our days, and banish all evils from thy Church: prosperously guide the steps, actions, and desires of us, and of all thy servants, in the way of salvation: give eternal blessings to our benefactors, and grant everlasting rest to all the faithful departed. Through our Lord Jesus Christ, thy Son, who liveth and reigneth with thee and the Holy Ghost, one God, world without end.
R. Amen.

Commemoration of the Saints in Advent

Ant. Behold, the Lord will come, and all his Saints with him:

and there shall be a great light on that day, Alleluia.

V. Behold, the Lord shall appear on a bright cloud.
R. And with him thousands of Saints.

Let us pray.

Cleanse our consciences, we beseech thee, O Lord, by thy holy visit, that when Jesus Christ, thy Son, our Lord, cometh with all his Saints, he may find in us an abode prepared for his reception: who liveth and reigneth with thee and the Holy Ghost, one God, world without end.
R. Amen.

After the commemoration for the Saints, the following Versicles are said, which conclude Vespers.

V. O Lord, hear my prayer
R. And let my cry come unto thee.

Or if a priest or deacon is presiding:

V. The Lord be with you.
R. And with thy Spirit.

Observe this at the end of each hour.

V. Let us bless the Lord.
R. Thanks be to God.

V. May the souls of the faithful departed, through the mercy of God, rest in peace.
R. Amen.

COMPLINE

Said at bedtime.

O divine and adorable Lord Jesus Christ, who has graciously redeemed us by thy bitter passion and death, we offer up these Compline to thy honor and glory, and most humbly beseech thee, through the injury thou didst suffer by the treacherous kiss of Judas, and by thy capture in the garden, to grant us thy grace that we may never betray thee by unworthily receiving the blessed sacraments, particularly the adorable Eucharist of thy body and blood, in the state of mortal sin, and that we may bridle our passions, and bind down our vicious inclinations under the sweet yoke and light burden of thy holy law till death. Amen.

Hail, Mary, full of grace, the Lord is with thee. Blessed art thou among women, and blessed is the fruit of thy womb, Jesus. Holy Mary, mother of God, pray for us sinners, now, and in the hour of our death. Amen.

V. Convert us to thee, O God, our Savior.
R. And turn away thy wrath from us.

V. Incline unto my aid, O God.
R. O Lord, make haste to help me.

Glory be to the Father, and to the Son, and to the Holy Ghost. As it was in the beginning, is now, and ever shall be, world without end. Amen, Alleluia.

During Lent: *Praise be to thee, O Lord, king of eternal glory.*

Psalm 129: Saepe Expugnaverunt.

Many times have they fought against me from my youth, let

91

Israel now say. Many times have they fought against me from my youth: but they could not prevail over me. The wicked have exerted their cruelty upon my back: they have prolonged their iniquity.

The Lord, who is just, will cut the neck of sinners: let them all be confounded and rejected, who hate Sion. Let them be as grass upon the tops of houses: which withered away before it was plucked up:
Wherewith the mower did not fill his hand: nor the gleaner his bosom.
And they who passed by have not said: The blessing of the Lord be upon you: we have blessed you in the name of the Lord.

Glory be to the Father, and to the Son, and to the Holy Ghost. As it was in the beginning, is now, and ever shall be, world without end. Amen, Alleluia.

Psalm 130: De Profundus.

From the deep I have cried out to thee; O gracious Lord, hear my voice. Let thy ears be attentive to the voice of my petition. If thou wilt consider our iniquities, O mighty Lord, who shall endure it?
But with thee there is merciful forgiveness: and by reason of thy law I have waited on thee, O Lord.

My soul hath relied on his word: my soul hath hoped in the Lord. From the morning watch even until night, let Israel hope in the Lord. Because with the Lord there is mercy: and with him plentiful redemption. And he shall redeem Israel from all his iniquities.

Glory be to the Father, and to the Son, and to the Holy Ghost. As it was in the beginning, is now, and ever shall be, world without end. Amen, Alleluia.

Psalm 131: Domine Non Est.

O Lord, my heart is not puffed up: nor are my eyes disdainful. Neither have I been ambitious of great affairs, nor have I dared to scrutinize in wonderful things above me. If I thought not humbly of myself; but proudly elevated my mind: Treat me as a nurse treats her infant, when she weans it from her breasts. Let Israel hope in the Lord, now and forevermore.

Glory be to the Father, and to the Son, and to the Holy Ghost. As it was in the beginning, is now, and ever shall be, world without end. Amen, Alleluia.

Hymn

Remember thou, Creator Lord,
The Father God's co-equal Word,
To save mankind, from Virgin's womb
Our human nature didst assume.

O happy Mary, full of grace,
Dear mother of the Prince of Peace,
Protect us from our evil foe,
And bliss, at death, on us bestow.

To thee, O Jesus, Mary's Son,
Be everlasting homage done;
To God the Father, we repeat
The same, and to the Paraclete.
Amen.

The Little Chapter through the year, except in Advent

Ecclesiasticus 24:24

I am the mother of beautiful love, and of fear, and of knowledge, and of holy hope.

R. Thanks be to God.
V. Pray for us, O holy Mother of God.
R. That we may be made worthy of the promises of Christ.

The Little Chapter in Advent

Isaiah 7:14

Behold, a virgin shall conceive and bring forth a Son, and his name shall be called Emmanuel. He shall eat butter and honey, that he may know how to reject evil and choose good.
R. Thanks be to God.

V. The angel of the Lord declared unto Mary.
R. and she conceived by the Holy Ghost.

(Through the year) Ant. Under thy protection we seek refuge, O holy Mother of God; despise not our petitions in our necessities, but deliver us continually from all dangers, O glorious and blessed virgin.

(Paschal time) Ant. O Queen of Heaven, rejoice, Alleluia, because he whom thou didst deserve to bear, Alleluia, is risen again, as he foretold, Alleluia: pray for us to God, Alleluia.

(In Advent) Ant. The Holy Ghost shall come upon thee, Mary: do not fear, thou shalt have in thy womb the Son of God, alleluia.

Compline

(Christmas time) Ant. Great is the mystery of our inheritance: the womb of a pure virgin became the temple of God: he, who took flesh of her, was not defiled: all nations shall come and say: Glory be to thee, O Lord.

Canticle of Simeon. Luke 2:29-32

Now dost thou dismiss thy servant, O Lord, according to thy word, in peace: Since my eyes have seen thy promised salvation. Which thou hast prepared to show to all nations; a light to enlighten the Gentiles, and the glory of thy people Israel.

(Through the year) Ant. Under thy protection we seek refuge, O holy Mother of God; despise not our petitions in our necessities, but deliver us continually from all dangers, O glorious and blessed virgin.

(Paschal time) Ant. O Queen of Heaven, rejoice, Alleluia, because he whom thou didst deserve to bear, Alleluia, is risen again, as he foretold, Alleluia: pray for us to God, Alleluia.

(In Advent) Ant. The Holy Ghost shall come upon thee, Mary: do not fear, thou shalt have in thy womb the Son of God, alleluia.

(Christmas time) Ant. Great is the mystery of our inheritance: the womb of a pure virgin became the temple of God: He, who took flesh of her, was not defiled: all nations shall come and say: Glory be to thee, O Lord.

Lord have mercy on us.
Christ, have mercy on us.
Lord, have mercy on us.
V. O Lord, hear my prayer.
R. And let my cry come unto thee.
Let us pray.

(Through the year) Grant, we beseech thee, O Lord, that the glorious intercession of the ever blessed and glorious Virgin Mary may protect us here, and bring us to everlasting life. Through our Lord Jesus Christ, thy Son: Who with thee and the Holy Ghost, liveth and reigneth one God, world without end.
R. Amen.

(In Advent) O God, who was pleased that thy Word, when the angel delivered his message, should take flesh in the womb of the blessed Virgin Mary; give ear to our humble petitions, and grant that we, who believe her to be truly the mother of God, may be helped by her prayers. Through the same Lord Jesus Christ, who with thee and the Holy Ghost liveth and reigneth one God, world without end. Amen.

(Christmas time) O God, who, by the fruitful virginity of blessed Mary, has given to mankind the rewards of eternal salvation; grant, we beseech thee, that we may experience her intercession, by whom we have deserved to receive the Author of life, our Lord Jesus Christ, thy Son: Who with thee and the Holy Ghost, liveth and reigneth one God, world without end. Amen.

V. O Lord, hear my prayer.
R. And let my cry come unto thee.
V. Let us bless the Lord.
R. Thanks be to God.

Blessing: May the almighty and merciful Lord, the Father, the Son, and the Holy Ghost, bless and protect us.
R. Amen.

Then one of the Antiphons of the Blessed Virgin Mary, according to the time of year.

ANTIPHONS

From Advent to the Purification

Mother of Jesus, heaven's open gate,
Star of the sea, support the falling state
Of mortals: thou, whose womb thy Maker bore,
And yet, O strange! A virgin, as before:
Who didst from Gabriel's hail the news receive,
Repenting sinners by thy prayers relieve.

V. The angel of the Lord declared unto Mary.
R. And she conceived by the Holy Ghost.

Let us pray.

Pour forth, we beseech thee, O Lord, thy grace into our hearts,
that we, to whom the incarnation of Christ, thy Son, was made
known by the message of an angel, may by his passion and
cross be brought to the glory of this resurrection: through the
same Christ our Lord. Amen.

V. After childbirth thou didst remain a pure virgin.
R. O Mother of God, intercede for us.

Let us pray.

O God, who by the fruitful virginity of blessed Mary, has
given to mankind the rewards of eternal salvation; grant, we
beseech thee, that we may experience her intercession, by
whom we receive the Author of life, our Lord Jesus Christ,
thy Son. Amen.

From The Purification until Holy Saturday

Hail Mary, Queen of heavenly spheres!
Hail, whom the angelic host reveres!
Hail, fruitful root! Hail, sacred gate!
From whom our light derives its date.
O glorious Maid, with beauty blest!
May joys eternal fill thy breast!
Thus crowned with beauty and with joy,
Thy prayers for us with Christ employ.

V. Vouchsafe, O sacred Virgin, to accept my praises.
R. Give me strength against thy enemies.

Let us pray.

Grant us, O merciful God, strength against all our weakness; that we, who celebrate the memory of the holy Mother of God, may by the help of her intercession rise again from our iniquities: through the same Christ, our Lord. Amen.

From Easter through the Saturday of Whitsunweek

Rejoice, O Queen of heaven, to see, alleluia,
The sacred infant born of thee, alleluia,
Return in glory from the tomb, alleluia:
And with thy prayers prevent our doom, alleluia.

V. Rejoice, and exult, O Virgin Mary, alleluia.
R. For the Lord is truly risen, alleluia.

Let us pray.

O God, who by the resurrection of thy Son, our Lord Jesus Christ, has been pleased to fill the world with joy; grant, we beseech thee, that by the intercession of the Virgin Mary, his mother, we may receive the joys of eternal life: through the same Christ, our Lord. Amen.

From Trinity Sunday eve to the beginning of Advent

Hail, happy Queen, thou mercy's parent, hail!
Life, hope, and comfort of this earthly vale.
To thee we, Eva's wretched children, cry,
In sighs and tears, to thee suppliants fly.
Rise, glorious advocate, exert thy love,
And let our vows those eyes of pity move.
O pious Virgin Mary, grant that we,
Long exiled, may in heaven thy Jesus see.

V. Pray for us, O holy mother of God.
R. That we may be made worthy of the promises of Christ.

Let us pray.

O Almighty and eternal God, who by the cooperation of the Holy Ghost, didst prepare the body and soul of the glorious Virgin Mary, that she might become a habitation worthy of thy Son; grant that, as with joy we celebrate her memory, so by her pious intercession we may be delivered form present evils and eternal death: Through the same Christ, our Lord. Amen.

After the proper Antiphon of the Blessed Virgin Mary, according to the time of year, is said the Versicle:

V. May the divine assistance always remain with us.
R. Amen.

Made in the USA
Monee, IL
22 September 2024

f7ccb4e5-f77c-4051-a3c3-868b0ba1881aR01